The
DIVORCE
Organizer & Planner
———————— Second Edition

The
DIVORCE
Organizer & Planner
Second Edition

Brette Sember, JD

New York   Chicago   San Francisco   Athens   London   Madrid
Mexico City   Milan   New Delhi   Singapore   Sydney   Toronto

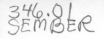
1 2 3 4 5 6 7 8 9 10 11 12 13 14 15 16 17   QVS/QVS   1 0 9 8 7 6 5 4 3

ISBN 978-0-07-182997-7 (book and CD set)
MHID 0-07-182997-0 (book and CD set)

ISBN 978-0-07-182993-9 (book for set)
MHID 0-07-182993-8 (book for set)

e-ISBN 978-0-07-182800-0
e-MHID 0-07-182800-1

Library of Congress Cataloging-in-Publication Data

Sember, Brette, 1968–
    The divorce organizer & planner / Brette Sember. 2nd edition
      p. cm.
    ISBN 0-07-182997-0
    Includes bibliographical references and index.
    1. Divorce suits—United States—Popular works.
    KF535.Z9 S46 2014
    346.7301'66
                                    2013026924

McGraw-Hill Education products are available at special quantity discounts to use as premiums and sales promotions or for use in corporate training programs. To contact a representative, please visit the Contact Us pages at www.mhprofessional.com.

"This publication is designed to provide accurate and authoritative information in regard to the subject matter covered. It is sold with the understanding that the publisher and author are not engaged in rendering legal, accounting, or other professional service. If legal advice or other expert assistance is required, the services of a competent professional person should be sought."
      —*From the Declaration of Principles jointly adopted by a Committee of the American Bar Association and a Committee of Publishers and Associations.*

This book is printed on acid-free paper.

Contents

Preface

Nothing about divorce is easy. You're going through emotional ups and downs, rearranging your living accommodations, dealing with financial problems, helping your kids cope, and trying to get through the confusing legal maze ahead of you. The last thing you probably want to do is focus on the nitty-gritty paperwork, but getting organized is one of the best ways to get through your divorce. Despite the many difficult emotions it involves, a divorce is really a business transaction. Business transactions that are handled in an organized and careful way tend to be successful. Because you are struggling with so many emotions during a divorce, it is often hard to think clearly, but you need a clear mind to ensure that you cover all the details. Getting what you want is often a function of presenting enough solid evidence to support your request, whether it is custody, child support, alimony, or a property settlement. This book will help you do that.

Divorces are all about paperwork. Everything except oral testimony must be presented to the court in writing. You will have to gather a lot of information about assets, debts, and property for your attorney, and you will have to organize it carefully. If you hand over an envelope stuffed with papers that have been thrown together, your attorney will have to spend time sorting through them, and you will be billed for that time. The more organized you are, the more you can reduce your attorney fees.

You also need to document issues such as visitation problems, household items that need to be divided, phone calls, names of people who can testify on your behalf, and so on. When you put the information on paper or in digital files, you can arrange it in an easy-to-follow format and present it to your attorney. If you don't write things down, you have to explain them from memory when you meet with your attorney or talk on the phone. You may not be sure if he or she understands what you're saying, and you might forget to mention some key points. This book helps you avoid miscommunication.

This may be one of the most confusing times in your life. Many people in your situation don't know what to do to improve their chances at obtaining custody or a better settlement. They are overwhelmed by the sheer amount of paperwork involved. Using the forms and organizational tools in this book, you will learn not only how to organize important documents and records, but also how to create logs that will help your attorney prove your case and get the outcome you desire. It is one thing to know that your spouse has violated a temporary order of visitation; it is quite another to be able to hand your attorney a detailed log containing the dates, times, and details of each violation. The more detailed your records are, the easier it is for your attorney to present your case to the court.

After you have worked your way through this book, you will have created a detailed record that your attorney can use to complete court documents and present your case effectively. You may want to use some of the forms in this book over and over again as you work through the divorce process. You may need to modify certain forms as your divorce progresses.

The book includes tips on how to select and work with an attorney, how to prepare yourself for court, what to do once your divorce is finalized, and much more. You will be well prepared for all of the meetings and court proceedings ahead of you. And you will find that being organized and prepared will make a huge difference in the way you feel, the expenses you incur, and the outcomes you get.

Acknowledgments

Special thanks to Janet Rosen and Sheree Bykofsky, agents extraordinaire, who were tireless in bringing this project to fruition. I am so grateful for all of your hard work. The book you are reading is in large part due to the skill and thoughtfulness of my editor Kathryn Keil. My gratitude goes out to the team at McGraw-Hill Education, including Nancy Hall, who worked around my schedule, put all the pieces together, and created this beautiful book!

How to Use This Book

This book is designed to be a get-organized tool to help you through the legal process of your divorce. The chapters tell you what documents and files you need to locate, access, and organize. They also explain how to use the forms that go with this book. All of this information is presented to help you organize information, facts, and your thoughts clearly, so you can give your attorney a well-organized and well-thought-out package of information. You're paying your attorney by the hour. Anything you can do to minimize the time you spend in his or her office or to reduce the time your attorney has to spend sorting through and organizing your documents is money you save.

The forms in this book will help you find and put together all the facts your attorney will need to handle your case. He or she will give you more forms to complete. In some cases, you will be able to attach a form you have used here to the attorney's form since it will contain all the information needed; in others, you can simply transfer the information from one form to the other. The downloadable forms can be saved and reused as many times as you need to.

This book is not meant to be read in one sitting. Instead, look at it as a long-term project. Start at the beginning and work your way through, gathering documents and information as you go. Ideally, you want to have all of the work in this book completed by the time you sit down with your attorney to file papers beginning your divorce, but it is OK to continue to work on this project over time, as your divorce moves forward.

This book is not meant as a do-it-yourself divorce guide. To file and handle your own divorce, you would need to get forms from your state (available on the state court website or at the courthouse) and do some research to understand your rights and options. Instead, this book is a support to help you stay on target as your attorney files and handles your divorce.

1

Getting and Staying Organized

Getting organized is the single most important thing you can do to ensure that your attorney will be able to represent you well, that the court will see your side of the story, and that you will be able to cope with your divorce and all the work it entails. Staying organized isn't always easy, but it is always helpful.

Dealing with Emotions

Your emotions are a major hurdle to remaining organized and developing a strategy for your divorce, which will be one of the most traumatic events of your life. You are going to feel confused, hurt, angry, frustrated, frightened, overloaded, and sad. It is hard to control your overpowering emotions when meeting with your lawyer, listening to half-truths and misrepresentations in court, communicating with your spouse and the opposing attorney, and facing all of the divorce-related paperwork. But these emotions will only get in the way of what is essentially a complicated business transaction.

The best thing you can do is to deal with your emotions so they don't interfere with the difficult work ahead. This doesn't mean you have to suppress your feelings. It does mean you should approach your divorce with a cool and calculated mindset that will allow you to keep clear records, deal with your attorney, negotiate with your spouse, and get through court appearances. You can't do that if your emotions are out of control. You're likely to miss things when you make emotional decisions.

Do whatever you need to do to get through the emotional part of your divorce—see a counselor, talk to friends, find new hobbies and new friends, spend time with your family, and so on—but don't allow your emotions to interfere with the careful planning and organizing you must do. Try to keep the business part of the divorce separate from the emotional part. The Resources section at the end of this book lists resources that can help you cope with these tangled feelings.

Deciding What You Want

Many people come to the divorce process still uncertain whether a divorce is the answer for them (and it's very common to change your mind about this several times). If you have any doubts, talk to your spouse and see a counselor or marriage therapist. You cannot proceed efficiently through the process if you are unsure whether divorce is the best avenue.

Decision making is an integral part of the divorce process. You need to determine what you want in terms of custody, alimony, child support, property division, and debt. This book will help you identify and organize all of the information that affects these key decisions. It won't help you determine what your goals are in the divorce. That is something you will need to think long and hard about.

Some of the decisions ahead will be very difficult to make, while others will seem obvious. You will change your mind about some decisions several times. You might not always find the perfect solution, simply because no perfect solution exists. Try to stay focused and tackle one decision at a time. Realize that while your choices are important, making a mistake is not the end of the world. Try to keep your perspective. No matter what happens, you will survive the divorce process and get on with your life.

Developing an Organizational System

This book is designed to help you organize the information that affects your divorce. You will find that to work with the system set up in this book, you have to make a commitment to being organized in all areas of your life.

Being organized will reduce your stress level and give you a feeling of control over the divorce process. (You can't control how your ex behaves, but at least you can have orderly spreadsheets or files!) It can also save you time and money as you go through the process. Your attorney will be able to hit the ground running and won't waste time collecting records that you can assemble yourself.

Being organized does not mean being anal or compulsive. It does, however, mean that you will have to devote some time to organizing and creating records. Once you understand what you need to do, it is easy to maintain the system.

To get organized, you need to develop routines that ensure you will keep information in the proper places. Make it a habit, for example, to record the date, time, and content of phone calls with your spouse. Make it second nature to pull up the phone log as soon as you hang up or refer to your recent call list to help you document this at the end of each day. Keep hard copy bills in the same place after paying them and track your online payments. Record child support payments when you write or deposit the checks or when the money is automatically withdrawn or deposited. Creating routines will help you keep records without having to think about it.

Saving Money Through Organization

Training yourself to remain organized throughout the divorce process will help you save money. Your attorney is paid by the hour (and is probably charging you $200 an hour or more). He or she bills in five-, ten-, or fifteen-minute increments and always rounds up! Your attorney charges for time in court or in a meeting, as well as for phone calls, e-mails, and time spent working on your file. Anything you do to reduce the amount of time he or she has to spend on your case will reduce your costs.

Attorneys spend a lot of time telling their divorce clients what documents they need to provide; how to keep records for visitation and child support; and how to create lists of assets, budgets, and so on. This book gives you a huge head start by helping you collect, organize, and record all of this information into a format that you can easily copy and give to your attorney. This will reduce your attorney's billable hours and save you money. Note that even if you think your ex is going to end up paying for your legal bills, it makes sense to try to reduce the amount of these bills. There is only one pot of money to be divided in your marriage. If you use some of it up unnecessarily on legal work, there's less left to divide.

Keeping a Calendar

You probably already keep a calendar for household or business appointments. Maybe you use a work calendar on your computer, tablet, or phone. You may have a wall calendar on which you and your family record school and sports events. But because your divorce is going to infiltrate every aspect of your life, you need to keep a master calendar on which you record everything. If you're already using a digital calendar, continue to use it. Note, however, that sometimes when working out visitation for children, it can be helpful to have a printout of the calendar that you and your ex can look at together and write possible scenarios on.

The master calendar will list your children's appointments; your personal and business appointments; and all your divorce-related meetings, court appearances, and deadlines. Having a master calendar is important because your meetings with attorneys and court appearances may sometimes conflict with your family or business obligations. You need to have everything in front of you when dates are being scheduled so you can immediately speak up and let everyone know when you are unavailable. It can help to color code this calendar: blue for work, green for children, brown for personal, red for court dates, and so on.

It's also important to keep a complete calendar to use as evidence, should you ever need to prove where you or your children were at certain times. Keeping track of school events you attend, as well as times the children are with you or your spouse, will give you a simple history of how you and your children spent your time. See Chapter 14 for more information about this.

Tips for Managing a Master Calendar

If you are a paper-calendar kind of person, you may not always carry it. If this is the case, make a point to update your hard copy calendar as often as possible when you've added appointments, events, and activities to your schedule.

When you record divorce-related matters on the calendar, make sure you clearly note the place and time of the appointment or appearance. Indicate what room number it will be held in and whether the time is a.m. or p.m. You can also use the calendar to record deadlines. Your attorney will give you papers to complete at several points along the way. Find out when he or she needs them and put that date on your calendar. Make sure you write a clear explanation! An abbreviated note that says "papers" might make sense to you now, but it won't be as clear in two weeks or a month.

Calendar Review

Check your calendar at the beginning of each week (either on Sunday or on Monday morning). Review what is scheduled or due in the coming week. This way you won't suddenly realize on Thursday night that you have to get a financial affidavit back to your attorney on Friday when you haven't even begun to work on it. Make it a point to check your calendar every morning so you know where you need to be that day and when. You may be certain that your mediation meeting is at four o'clock when it was really scheduled for two o'clock. It's easy to mix up times and dates in the course of your normal, busy life, but it's even easier to do when you're under emotional stress.

Some people have a tendency to forget appointments or confuse times for things they dread or are uncomfortable about. If this is the case for you, you'll have to work extra hard to stay on top of things. Judges are rather unforgiving when it comes to scheduling mistakes. Set up reminders on your phone, computer, or tablet, so you will get several nudges about important court dates and appointments.

Using To-Do Lists

Some people are natural list makers, while others never use such reminders. Whichever category you fall into, you'll find that making lists is an efficient way to help you get things done and stay organized during your divorce. You're going to have a lot of details to deal with, and the best way to keep track of them is to put them in writing. Lists ease the strain of trying to remember every detail. Your list can be your memory. Use paper lists or create them digitally—whatever you prefer. (See the sample To-Do List at the end of this chapter.)

Types of To-Do Lists

There are lots of ways to structure to-do lists. You'll need to choose the types that work best for you.

Daily or Weekly Lists

Some people find that making a list of everything that has to get done on a certain day or during a week helps them stay focused and on target. Having a long list of things to get done over the course of a month or a few weeks doesn't help you find a way to move through the list. Breaking down the tasks and assigning a time in which each will be completed helps you get things done in an orderly way and manage your time so you can fit everything into your schedule. A sample daily list might include the following:

- Bring home insurance application from office desk
- Call Mom about babysitting
- Call lawyer about changing the locks
- Go to bank

You might find it helpful to make a master list of everything you need to do in a certain week and then assign the items on that list to specific days. That way if you don't get through your daily list, the item still appears on the weekly list and won't be forgotten.

Topic-Oriented Lists

Sometimes it's helpful to make lists organized by topics. For example, you might make one that focuses on household duties and include items like these:

- Get out box of memorabilia to divide
- Pick up empty boxes
- Call real-estate agent
- Mow lawn

Another list might be for divorce paperwork:

- Download missing credit card statement
- Find 401(k) papers
- Locate marriage license
- Make copies of kids' Social Security cards

Managing To-Do Lists

It's easy to make to-do lists and then forget about them, but these lists will work only if you use them. Keep your list where you can see it, and cross things off when you complete them. Check the list regularly so you don't forget any items. Make sure to keep your list in the most useful place. It will do you no good to make a list on your phone if you never check it. A paper list that sits someplace where you can't miss it can be the most effective for some people. You might also find that putting sticky notes in places where you can't miss them (your computer, the fridge, the bathroom mirror) can be an effective way to stay on track.

To increase the effectiveness of your lists, you may wish to keep them with your master calendar. You can coordinate your weekly

5

DIGITAL REMINDERS

It may be helpful to set digital reminders for yourself. You can schedule them so you are reminded to do something the day before or a few hours before. You can also schedule reminders of appointments, so you won't forget them.

activities and manage your to-do list at the same time. A blank to-do list is included in the forms for this book (on the CD or electronic forms are available for download for e-book readers).

Managing Documents

You're going to be up to your ears in paperwork and documents as you go through your divorce. Not only will there be correspondence and forms from your attorney, but there will also be lots of things you'll be solely responsible for, such as name changes on accounts, notifications to schools, and everything else involved in separating one set of finances into two.

It can be overwhelming to deal with all the forms, online forms, e-mails, files, and papers that will come your way during the process, but if you develop a system that lets you take control of them, you'll feel calmer. You'll also feel confident that everything is in a place where you can easily find it.

Accordion Folders

You need to keep track of court papers, of course, but you should also keep track of papers related to household expenses, income, debts, items you own, and more. If you keep hard copies of most of these records, purchase an accordion-style folder to use in conjunction with this book. Try to buy a plastic one. Since you will be carrying it with you to meetings and appointments, you want it to be sturdy. You may need to purchase two folders if you can't find one with enough pockets—you will need at least sixteen. You can also use a plastic box with file folders. (File boxes and accordion folders can be found at office supply stores.) Take the file with you to every meeting with your attorney and every court appearance. As you use this book, you will file papers in the folder and have them readily available so you can find what you need quickly. Label the dividers in your folder with the following headings:

Household Inventory
Documents to Complete for Attorney
Documents from Attorney/Court Papers
Attorney Bills and Receipts
Documents from Other Professionals
Household Documents
Income Documents
Monthly Expenses
Large Assets
Debts
Children's Expenses
Children's Uninsured Health Care Receipts
Child Support Receipts

Alimony Receipts
Evidence from Witnesses
Property Distribution Receipts

As you work through this book, you will learn how to use each pocket.

Digital Management

If you keep most of your records as digital files, you need to get those organized as well. Create a folder for each category listed in the previous section, and plan to create subfolders within these as we move through the book; for example, you will likely have several subfolders under Monthly Expenses, such as Gas Bills, Phone Bills, and so on). Develop a system for naming documents that will make it easy for you to find them in the future. For example, in the digital folder for your children's uninsured health care expenses, save each receipt using the name of the doctor or facility and the date, such as BrewerNov2014. Always include a date in the file name. Not only will this make it easier to find items, but it will help you identify the most recent versions of documents such as court orders or bills.

Make sure to bring all these files with you on your computer, your tablet, or a jump drive when you go to any meeting or appearance with your attorney.

Household Paperwork

You probably already have some kind of system in place for managing household paperwork, but because so many of the documents it contains are going to be important in your divorce, take a minute to think about that system.

If you haven't done so yet, identify one specific place where you will put all your important hard copy papers. You know how it is when you open the mail or your children hand you papers from school. You set the information aside until you have time to deal with it, but things are easily lost or forgotten this way. Pick one place where you will put incoming mail. A wire basket works well, as does a spot on a desk, counter, or bookcase.

Go through the stack once a week to pay bills and fill out forms that are due. Then file everything else where you can find it again easily. A two-drawer file cabinet is ideal for this. Label a folder for every company or organization you deal with, such as the electric company, school, cable company, health insurance carrier, bank, and so on.

If you don't have a file cabinet, use a plastic box with file folders in it or an expandable file folder with compartments that can be labeled. It doesn't matter where you put the papers, as long as you put them somewhere. It's important to distinguish between old and new accounts. For example, if the electric bill was in both names and is now in one name only, start a separate file for the single account. Do the same thing for credit cards, bank accounts, and so on. Create labels that are specific to what is in the file. For example, electric bills should be filed under the name of the company, not under *L* for "lights." Using appropriate labels will make your documents easier to find.

Remember, this is filing for your own personal use for your household organization. You will remove documents from this system and move them into your accordion file if you need them for your divorce.

E-mails and Online Documents

If you receive household bills, statements, or important correspondence via e-mail or view such documents online, you need to make sure you have a method for saving it. Create separate folders within your e-mail program for statements and correspondence you need to keep. If you view bills and statements online, you need to save them in a folder where you can locate them easily. As suggested earlier, make sure you label each file in a way that will allow you to find it and include the date. If you're viewing and paying bills online, make it part of your routine to download a copy of the statement or bill every time you pay it.

Be honest about your ability to manage digital documents. If you find yourself forgetting to make payments, the chances that you will remember to download the bills for your records are slim. Switch to mailed statements if you find you're not keeping up with this.

When you need to access these files for your divorce, copy them and move a copy to the digital file you are keeping with divorce documents. Make sure you leave a copy in your normal household folder.

Other General Organizational Tips

Here are a few more organizational and self-management tips to help you move through the divorce process:

- **Always leave early for appointments.** You may have trouble finding the courthouse or nearby parking. You don't want to be late.
- **Continue to eat and drink on a normal schedule.** You will feel out of sorts and confused if you skip meals.
- **Retain normalcy in your life.** Go to the gym, have dinner with the kids, go out with friends, and take care of household chores. Keeping a routine will help you stay focused and feel like you are living a normal life.
- **Try to maintain a nonconfrontational attitude with your spouse.** Divorce is all about conflict, but if you can minimize the disputes, you will feel less stressed out and better able to cope with the ones that can't be avoided.
- **Take the issues involved in your divorce one at a time, and focus on solutions rather than problems.** If you look at the divorce as a whole, it can seem overwhelming, but if you deal with one step at a time, it will be more manageable.
- **Stop looking behind you.** You can't change the past, but you can deal with the present and plan for the future. Focus on what you *can* affect.

- **Give yourself a break.** You're not perfect, and you're even less likely to be perfect when you're going through a divorce. If you expect too much of yourself, you're going to feel let down if you can't meet those high expectations.
- **Don't make everything into a crisis.** Take a step back and try to get some perspective. Remember, this is just one small section of your life, and it will be over soon.
- **Develop routines that will help you get things done.** Always do the laundry on Monday nights, set out lunch money the night before, put your keys in one place, and so on. Even if you were not a routine-oriented person before the divorce, try to be one now.
- **Be in charge of your divorce; don't let your divorce be in charge of you.** This book helps you grab the reins and direct the process. Don't let yourself fall into passivity. Make decisions, take action, and ask questions.

TO-DO LIST

Print copies of this list for further use.

To-Do List for _____ **[day or week]**

2

Protecting Yourself

No matter how amicable your divorce is (or seems), you must prepare yourself for the worst. Many people start a divorce thinking it will be fast and friendly, only to find out that their spouse is using underhanded tactics, isn't being completely honest, or is breaking agreements. People change when they go through a divorce, so while you and your spouse may have decided to part on amiable terms, he or she could change. Suddenly, your friendly divorce could turn into a battle.

Protecting yourself means planning for the worst while hoping for the best. You can take steps to protect your financial security and your children while at the same time being cooperative and agreeable with your spouse. You can rest assured that if your spouse has an attorney (and often even if he or she doesn't), he or she is taking similar defensive measures. Protecting yourself doesn't mean you have to be sneaky, devious, mean, or money hungry. It does mean that you put yourself and your kids first.

You're on your own now. You have to look out for yourself. You relied on your spouse in the past, but you can't do so anymore.

Dealing with Money

You probably have many different joint accounts with your spouse—bank accounts, credit cards, loans, and so on. The first step in protecting yourself is to make sure your spouse can't create financial problems for you.

Cash

Make sure you have some cash on hand. If your bank accounts and credit cards are frozen (which can happen if the judge decides to do so or if your spouse freezes the credit cards), you will need money. Withdraw enough cash to get you through at least two weeks without using a credit card, debit card, or check. Keep it someplace safe and use it only in an emergency.

Bank Accounts

If you don't have a separate bank account in your own name, it's time to open one. You can do so with as little as a dollar. What's important is opening it—not how much you have in it. You need to establish your own credit and your own financial system.

Next, you need to take a look at your joint checking and savings accounts. The best plan of action is to agree with your spouse to close these accounts and split the cash. Another choice is to keep one joint account functioning and use it to pay household expenses (for a jointly owned home) until the divorce is resolved. If you do this, you must agree how much each of you will deposit on a regular basis, and you must trust that your spouse will not use this money for other things.

You both have the right to withdraw all the funds from a joint account at any time without the other's permission, whether it contains $10 or $10,000. If you're worried, take half of the money from the account and place it in a separate account. This way you will have access to your half no matter what. Your spouse's attorney may object, but if it is clear you have placed this money in an account for safekeeping and not with the intent to spend it all on yourself, it won't be a problem. Make sure you consult your own attorney before making *any* decisions about bank accounts. Your attorney can ask the judge to issue a temporary order determining who has access to which accounts or freezing certain accounts. While this is the safest course of action, it takes time; if you're worried about the money disappearing, withdrawing half may be the best solution in the short term. It's a good idea to monitor activity in joint bank accounts online on a regular basis until they are finally divided or closed. Be sure to change the password for your ATM card as well. If you have automatic withdrawals set up for utilities or rent or mortgage payments on the marital home, you need to either leave enough in the account to cover them, or you need to change your settings and set these accounts up for manual payment (via check in the mail).

Direct Deposit

If your paycheck or other funds (even things like PayPal or eBay payments) are deposited directly into a joint account, you need to change this so that the funds now go to your separate account.

Credit Cards

Either of you can charge anything to joint cards, and the credit card company will hold both of you responsible. If your spouse refuses to pay or goes bankrupt, you're on the hook for the entire amount, even if you aren't the one who charged the item and didn't know about it. If you use the card and don't pay the balance, your spouse can ask the court to order you to pay it. Either way, using joint cards complicates things and increases attorney fees.

Because of this joint liability, it's essential to close your joint accounts as soon as possible and open new accounts in your own name. If you have remaining balances on the joint cards, you can do one of two things: you can each transfer a portion of the debt to individual accounts and pay them off separately, or you can leave the joint account open

> ## FLEXIBLE SPENDING ACCOUNTS
>
> Flexible spending accounts (FSAs), as well as health savings accounts (HSAs), are joint property no matter whose name they are in. Talk to your attorney about how to use these accounts while your divorce is in progress.

but instruct the credit card company that no new charges can be made on it. The latter course freezes the account (and requires both of you to agree to unfreeze it) until the divorce settlement sorts out who will be responsible for it. Once the court decides this, you need to transfer the balance to solo accounts or pay it off immediately, because even if a court orders that your spouse is responsible for a joint account balance, it won't stop the credit card company from coming after you if payment is not made. Note also that even if the account is frozen, interest will continue to accrue if the balance is not paid off.

Be sure to change the credit card numbers on all accounts that automatically charge your cards, such as subscriptions, online shopping accounts such as Amazon, or utilities. Monitor joint credit cards online on a regular basis to be certain your ex isn't misusing them. If you have existing credit card accounts in your name only, be sure to change the online log-in passwords.

If your divorce drags on for more than a year, it may be a good idea to order your credit report every five or six months to make sure your spouse has not applied for a joint credit card or loan without your consent.

Credit Report

You are entitled to one free copy of your credit report from each of the three credit reporting agencies. You can order them all via the government site https://www.annual creditreport.com, or you can contact each company individually using the following information:

Experian
888-397-3742
http://www.experian.com

TransUnion
P.O. Box 105281
Atlanta, GA 30348-5281
877-322-8228
http://www.transunion.com

Equifax
P.O. Box 740241
Atlanta, GA 30374
800-685-1111
http://www.equifax.com

Your credit report will list all credit cards and loans in your name (including those that are held jointly). You can close accounts that are open but inactive to prevent future abuse by your spouse, and you'll find out if your spouse has opened any new joint accounts without your knowledge. You'll also get your credit score and see if you are delinquent on any accounts. You're not entitled to a copy of your spouse's report; only he or she can obtain that.

Joint Investments

As soon as you begin divorce proceedings, freeze all your joint investment accounts so nothing can be withdrawn from them and loans can't be placed against them. As with cash, you could remove half and place it in an account for safekeeping, but it is best to discuss this strategy with your attorney. As with other accounts, while they are open, you should be monitoring their activity online.

Children's Accounts

If you have children and they have bank accounts, investments, or college savings plans, these may be joint accounts with you or your spouse. If your spouse's name is on the accounts, there is nothing you can do on your own to prevent him or her from draining them. Get copies of the account statements (you can't get these from the bank if you're not on the account and will have to locate copies at home or access the accounts online using your spouse's passwords); let your attorney know about the accounts so that he or she can ask the court to freeze them. If your name appears on the accounts, make sure you leave them intact during the divorce proceedings.

Retirement Accounts

If your spouse has one or more retirement accounts (including 401(k)s and IRAs) in his or her name, contact the plan administrator for a copy of the brochure, plan, or summary, as well as a current account statement. Since you are not an account owner, you are not technically entitled to this, but as the spouse, the company may send it to you. If you cannot obtain it, you need to locate documents at home or access them online. You will want documentation of what is in the account and how the plan works. A retirement account (the portion of it accrued during the marriage) will be taken into consideration in a property settlement. You may want to take a cash settlement, or collect a portion of the payments when your spouse retires. See Chapter 9 for more information about retirement accounts.

Change the password for your own retirement accounts online.

Safe-Deposit Boxes

If you have a joint safe-deposit box that holds cash or assets, ask the bank to require both signatures to open the box. Use the Safe-Deposit Box Inventory form at the end of this chapter to create a record of everything in the box. Your other choice is to take out half of the cash or valuables in the box to protect yourself; you can also remove all important papers and place them in your own safe-deposit box. Consult your attorney about this.

Bills

Your household bills may be joint or sole accounts. If they are joint and you move out of the home, make sure your name is removed from the accounts; otherwise, you will continue to be responsible for them. You do not want to turn the utilities off if your spouse is still living in the home (this will be viewed as an unpleasant tactic by the court), but you do want to make sure you are no longer financially liable. If you aren't sure how to do this, call the utility companies and ask.

If the bills are in your spouse's name and he or she has moved out of the home, consider having the accounts transferred to your name so that your spouse cannot have the utilities turned off (also be sure to change the user name and password on each account). Note, however, that doing so will make you completely responsible for paying the bills, whereas if they are in your spouse's name, he or she bears the responsibility. Discuss the implications of this issue with your attorney. It is possible that the court could order your spouse to pay these bills, so be sure to ask.

The Home

Physically separating can bring a lot of relief from fighting, but when and how to separate is an important strategic decision. If you move out and leave the children with the other parent, you are setting things up for him or her to have custody. Additionally, if you move out, it decreases the chance that you will get possession of the home. For these reasons, it is a good idea to talk to your attorney before you decide to move out. Don't make the decision in a fit of anger.

Despite these caveats, there are times when living in the same house becomes unbearable and moving out is the only choice you have to keep everyone safe and sane. If this happens, talk to your attorney as soon as possible to see what you can do to protect your rights after the fact. Try to wait until you can ask the court for a temporary order directing exclusive occupancy of the home to one of you.

If one of you does move out, you'll want to record this date on your master calendar. (You might think you don't need a reminder of when this happened, but it's a good idea to document it!) The date of separation will matter when assets are divided by the court.

Household Belongings

Use the Household Belongings Inventory form to document and describe the more valuable objects you and your spouse own. Write down serial numbers for items that have them. Copy title and registration papers for cars that you and your spouse drive. Photograph or videotape all valuable items. Save all the photos or videos into one file and add captions with the dates they were taken. You can print out copies of the photos if you would like hard copy, and store the photos in the "Household Inventory" pocket of your accordion file. Items to photograph and document include the following:

- Jewelry
- Electronics (televisions, gaming systems, computers, and so on)
- Vehicles
- Valuable collections
- Antiques
- Valuable furniture and household items
- Other items worth more than $500

Mail

Even if you're not moving, open a post office box in your name alone for snail mail. You can request that your attorney and other professionals involved in the case send correspondence to you there if they need to. This way your spouse cannot access any of your postal mail, and you don't have to worry that he or she will read it or take it. Even if you have physically separated, your mail is not necessarily secure. It is easy for mail to be removed from your home or roadside box without your knowledge. A post office box is a good idea if you have any concerns about security or privacy.

Home Security

16

If your spouse has moved out and the court has given you sole occupancy, change the locks (if you are a renter, you may need your landlord's permission or will at least need to give him or her a key). Your ex is still an owner of the home, but you have possession. Reset your home security system with a new code and take your spouse's name off the account.

Change where you hide the spare key to the house. If there are any unsecured windows or doors, make sure they are repaired and secured. Ask that your spouse return garage door openers. If your garage door is programmed into your cars, change the code on the opener.

Keys

Request that your spouse return his or her keys and remotes to your car or vehicle, if the court has not already ordered him or her to do so. It's expensive to get the locks changed, so try your best to get the keys back.

If your spouse has keys to your parents' home or to that of another relative, ask for those back as well. If you have a home safe, give your spouse any items that belong to him or her from the safe and ask for the key back. If the safe uses a keypad or combination, contact the manufacturer for instructions on changing the code or combination.

Insurance

Consider switching your auto insurance from a joint policy to an individual policy. Since you will no longer be driving each other's cars, there's no reason to continue a joint policy. You will lose your multicar discount (if you have one) and may pay more, but you won't have to worry about facing a rate increase if your spouse has an accident. If ownership of the cars is going to be in question, you may need to continue joint insurance to protect both of your interests until the court determines ownership.

If you have only one car, you will need a court order to determine who will keep it if you can't agree. Remember that even if the car is in only one spouse's name, the other spouse can be given possession of it if it is a marital asset (purchased during the marriage). If you are given possession of the car, make sure you are listed as an authorized driver with the insurance company. If you're not, ask your spouse to change this. If he or she refuses, your attorney should ask the court to order him or her to do so. When your divorce is finalized, permanent ownership will be decided. If you get the car at that point, title will be transferred to you, and you will need to obtain your own insurance policy.

If your spouse is your life insurance beneficiary, contact your agent and complete a change of beneficiary form.

If you have moved out of the home, keep your name on the homeowner's insurance policy until the court makes a final decision about ownership. You're still an owner, and you want to protect that investment. If you and your spouse are renters and you move out of the residence, make sure the renter's insurance is kept in force as a joint policy, thus protecting any items that are yours or will be yours after the divorce is settled. If you move out of the home and become a renter, make sure you obtain a renter's policy for your new residence.

If you are remaining in the home, contact the insurance company and make sure they use only your contact information and do not cancel the homeowner's or renter's policy without your permission.

Electronics and Digital Life

You will need to change the user name and password for your e-mail account (or you can simply close your account and open a new one elsewhere). It is also a good idea to install a password on your computer, tablet, and phone so your spouse cannot even turn it on, let alone access anything you have on it. If you're still living in the same home, you need to get into the habit of closing your e-mail program and turning off your computer and other electronics between uses. You should also change the codes for your voice mail.

As painful as it may be, this is also the time to reset *all* of your passwords for everything, which can include any or all of the following:

- Netflix and other media streaming
- Amazon and anywhere else you shop online where you have an account set up
- Spotify and other streaming radio
- Instagram and other photo-sharing sites
- iTunes
- Facebook, Google+, Pinterest, Twitter, and all other social media
- Skype and any other video chatting
- Carbonite or any other computer backup services you use, such as iCloud
- LastPass or other password storage services
- Online medical chart passwords
- Pharmacy prescription renewal accounts
- Professional memberships
- Message boards, chat rooms, and other online communication tools
- Loyalty and frequent flyer programs
- Health, dental, life, auto, and homeowner's/renter's insurance log-ins

It can be very hard to remember all of your online accounts, so start changing them as you use them. If you already have a password storage system like LastPass, use this to go through the list and change everything.

Keep in mind that you and your ex probably know each other's common passwords, so think outside the box and come up with something completely new that he or she would never guess.

Something else you must think about now is how much of your life is available for view on social media sites. If adultery or custody is an issue in your divorce, or if your treatment of your spouse will be scrutinized by the court (and in some states, if you might be paying alimony, the court can look at your "bad behavior" during marriage to increase the award), then it's time for you to think long and hard about social media.

First, go through *all* of your postings and photos from the past year. Delete anything that could show you in a bad light. Change your privacy settings to restrict your future personal postings to close friends you trust the most. Unfriend your spouse immediately, and also consider unfriending his or her family and friends. Think twice in the future before posting anything that could give your spouse additional ammunition against you.

Cell Phones

If you and your ex have your cells on the same account, you will need to talk to your provider to find out if the account can be cancelled and two new accounts set up. If you have a long-term contract, this can be tricky, so be sure to talk to a representative and find out your options. At the very least, change your voice mail password.

If your ex has posted anything on social media that will help *your* case, print it and/ or take screenshots of it, so you have a copy if he or she deletes it.

Wills

Changing your will is one thing that will definitely be on your to-do list, but while you're still married, you will not completely cut ties with your spouse in this way. If you die while still married, in most states, your spouse gets a share of your estate no matter what your will says. It is a good idea, though, to obtain a copy of your will and make an appointment with your attorney to change it so that it will be in place after your divorce. You'll also want to think about guardianship for your children. In most cases, the children would live with the other parent if you die, but if you want to avoid this, you'll need a guardianship clause in your will. See Chapter 17 for more information about this topic.

Power of Attorney

If you have executed a power of attorney that gives your spouse the authority to handle financial or business affairs on your behalf, destroy it, revoke it in writing, or create a new one that supersedes the old one. Send a copy of the new form to any company or person who has one on file (such as your bank). Since power of attorney forms vary by state, check with your attorney to be sure you are using the proper form.

SOCIAL MEDIA POSTINGS TO DELETE OR AVOID IN THE FUTURE

The following are the types of things you should avoid posting on your social media accounts before your divorce is final:

- Photos or videos of you with people of the opposite sex that appear compromising in any way
- Posts that indicate or imply you have had an adulterous relationship
- Any references to drinking, drugs, or any illegal or questionable activities
- Any references to your child that could be construed as negative or showing poor judgment, and anything that paints you as a less-than-ideal parent
- Photos or videos that call into question the cleanliness or safety of your home, vehicles, or surroundings
- Posts, photos, or videos that suggest you are unstable, depressed, or of questionable mental health
- Threats against your ex or anything that could be construed that way, particularly anything implying you will keep your ex away from your child
- "Likes" of sites or pages that have anything to do with alcohol, drugs, criminal activity, violence, or anything your ex could turn against you in any way
- Photos or posts you wouldn't want your grandma, your minister, or your child to see

This is a good rule of thumb to help guide you as you navigate the divorce.

Health Care Directives

Sometimes called health care powers of attorney, living wills, or health care proxies, health care directives are documents that give another person the authority to make health care decisions for you should you ever be in a situation where you are unable to make your own decisions. You need to destroy or amend any health care directive that lists your spouse as the person having this authority on your behalf. Talk to your attorney about completing a new form (some doctors' offices can even provide this), and make sure you send copies of the new document to your doctors and any other health care provider who has a copy of your old form.

Physical Safety

If you have been physically abused or threatened by your spouse, or you fear that he or she will abuse or harm you, you first need to protect yourself physically and then worry about assets and belongings. If you are in danger, get to a domestic violence shelter immediately or call 911. If you don't feel you are in immediate danger but are still afraid, ask your attorney about obtaining an order of protection or a restraining order against your spouse. Keep the number for your closest domestic violence shelter in your phone, but remember that you should always call 911 first if you are threatened, because you will get an immediate response and protection from the local police. They can then help you get to a shelter or a safe place.

Protecting Your Children

If your children have been abused by your spouse, call your state's child abuse hotline (if you cannot find this online, call the national hotline at 1-800-4-A-CHILD). If your children are in immediate danger, you need to get them out of harm's way first and worry about everything else later. Contact your local domestic violence shelter or your local department of social services (or department of child and family services) for information about what to do and where to go. If you witness abuse or believe it has just happened, call the police.

20

If you are concerned about parental kidnapping, talk to your attorney and get a temporary order of custody. Then notify all schools and child care providers that your child is to be released only to you. Give them a copy of the court order. If your child has a passport, keep it in a safe-deposit box that your spouse cannot access. Only one passport can be issued per person, and without it, your child cannot legally be taken out of the country. Keep recent photos and fingerprints of your child in case they are ever needed (state police can provide home fingerprint kits, or you can go to their barracks and have it done). Use the Self-Protection Checklist form to make sure you have taken all necessary steps to protect yourself and your children.

Pets

Pets are legally considered to be another type of household possession, even though they are like children for many people. If there is a dispute over where your pets will live, you can get a temporary order from the court deciding where they will stay. If you are worried about your pets' safety, keep them in the house with you when you can't be outside to supervise them. Notify your vet or pet day care provider that only you are authorized to pick up your pet.

SAFE-DEPOSIT BOX INVENTORY

Box #_____

Financial Institution _____

Contents as of _____ (date)

_____
_____
_____
_____
_____
_____
_____
_____
_____
_____
_____
_____
_____
_____
_____
_____
_____
_____
_____
_____
_____
_____
_____
_____

HOUSEHOLD BELONGINGS INVENTORY

Description and Serial Number	Location	Approximate Value

SELF-PROTECTION CHECKLIST

- [ ] Keep cash on hand.
- [ ] Withdraw from or protect your joint bank accounts (and change your ATM password).
- [ ] Close or freeze joint credit cards.
- [ ] Obtain a copy of your credit report.
- [ ] Remove items from a joint safe-deposit box.
- [ ] Obtain a post office box.
- [ ] Secure your home. (Change the security code, make sure all windows and doors lock, change the hiding place for your spare key, and change the locks.)
- [ ] Change your voice mail password.
- [ ] Change your passwords for e-mail and all online accounts (including social media, shopping, medical services, credit cards, banking, and investment accounts).
- [ ] Obtain extra keys from your spouse for cars and relatives' homes, as well as garage door openers.
- [ ] Change your auto insurance.
- [ ] Change your life insurance beneficiary.
- [ ] Maintain homeowner's or renter's insurance.
- [ ] Obtain a copy of your will.
- [ ] Change powers of attorney.
- [ ] Change health care directives.
- [ ] Evaluate your physical safety and the safety of your children.
- [ ] Take steps to ensure pets' safety.

3

Working with an Attorney and Other Professionals

If you don't already have an attorney, it is important that you get one as soon as you (or your spouse) decide that you are going to get a divorce. If you have not made the decision to divorce yet and are on the fence, a lawyer can help you understand the process, the costs, your rights, and the possible outcomes. Some divorces can be handled without an attorney, but in a contested divorce (one in which your spouse has an attorney and you are not going to agree to everything he or she asks for), you will be best served by having your own representation. Even if you will be using mediation or collaborative law, you will need to have an attorney.

The legal profession is sometimes painted negatively, but you need an attorney to protect yourself in a divorce. Would you want to head into surgery without a surgeon on your case? A knowledgeable attorney is your best asset in a divorce. Most attorneys are honest and hardworking, but if you have a hard time trusting them, you need to work extra hard to find one you can trust and connect with. You're going to spend a lot of time with this person and rely on him or her for important advice, so be choosy.

Finding Legal Representation

If you have used an attorney in the past for speeding tickets or real estate, you might ask him or her for a referral to someone whose practice focuses on divorce. It is important to use an attorney who is experienced in handling divorces. You wouldn't hire your family doctor to operate on your heart, even though he or she might know something about cardiac surgery. You want an expert—someone who knows all the tricks of the trade and has a lot of experience in that area (someone who knows the other divorce attorneys and the judges and understands how things operate in your area).

ONLINE DIVORCE FILING SITES

The Internet is filled with websites that promise to file your divorce for you for a few hundred dollars. While this sounds like a simple way to get through the process without racking up a lot of legal bills, it is often a huge mistake. Divorce is complicated. If you have assets or children, or if child support or alimony may be an issue, you need an attorney who can spend time learning about all the details of your situation and work with you on a one-to-one basis. Everyone's case is different, and it is essential that you have good advice before making financial decisions.

Additionally, some sites file generic forms—forms they use in all states—and your local judge may decide not to accept them. Online sites do not talk with you about your rights, see things you might be missing, explain your state laws to you, or analyze what you might be entitled to. Getting in-person legal advice is always a good idea in a divorce.

Referrals are a great way to find an attorney with whom you can build a good working relationship. Ask friends and relatives for suggestions (use your online social network to reach the largest number of people), or check your city, county, or state bar association website. Most have programs that will refer you to an experienced divorce attorney in your area, and you can probably plug in your location and issue and get a name immediately. The American Academy of Matrimonial Lawyers can also provide referrals online or over the phone (http://www.aaml.org; 312-263-6477). Once you have the name of an attorney, you can get some basic information about him or her by checking the website of your state bar association or state attorney registration, or by looking in the Martindale-Hubbell directory (available at libraries in book format or online at http://www.martindale.com). It can also be helpful just to Google the attorney to find out what people are saying about him or her and if he or she has had any noteworthy cases recently. Be sure to read his or her website to get a feel for what the person and practice is like. Check to see if there are client intake forms you can download and take to your appointment. You may also be able to set up your initial appointment through e-mail.

Questions to Ask an Attorney

Once you have a referral to an attorney, schedule a free consultation. You can't be charged for anything until you agree to a fee, and most attorneys will be willing to talk with you for a short time to help you understand the basics of how the case will go. Go to the appointment prepared to ask questions and determine if this is the right representative for you. Don't be intimidated. Before you purchase a new car, you ask a lot of questions and take it for a test drive. Why should this be any different? The following questions can help you determine if the attorney you talk to is someone you want to handle your divorce.

Questions to Ask Yourself
- Was I able to get an initial appointment quickly?
- Was the office staff friendly and efficient when I contacted them by phone or online?

- Do I feel comfortable in the waiting room?
- Are the office personnel friendly and polite in person?
- Does the office appear organized?
- Does the atmosphere seem frantic or calm?
- Am I being kept waiting longer than I'm comfortable with?
- Is parking nearby and convenient?
- Is the office convenient to my home or workplace?

Questions to Ask the Attorney

- **Where did you go to law school?** The answer isn't terribly important, but if he or she went to a school overseas or to one you've never heard of, you should be wary.
- **How long have you been practicing this type of law?** Look for an attorney who has been practicing family law for at least several years. Many lawyers who have a general practice do handle divorces, and you may feel comfortable with someone like this, but be aware that there are those who focus solely on divorce and family law and thus will have more experience (and are likely to charge more).
- **How many divorce cases have you handled in the past six months?** Look for someone who has handled at least ten in the last six months.
- **What are your fees?** Find out what he or she charges for expenses such as copying, phone calls, and paralegal work.
- **What is your hourly rate?** Fees vary across the country, but you should expect to be charged $150 an hour or more. The more experienced the attorney, the higher the fee. It is also common to charge a higher hourly rate for time spent in court. Find out if you will be charged for travel time to and from the courthouse.
- **Is there a retainer fee?** A retainer fee is like a down payment you make when you agree to hire the attorney. Expect one, but make sure it is an amount you can afford. The attorney bills against the retainer, and any unused portion is refundable.
- **How much are the court fees?** Court filing fees will vary from state to state. If you have concerns about the fees you are quoted, call your local bar association for confirmation or check your state court website.
- **Can I get my spouse to pay the court fees and part or all of the attorney fees?** This will depend on your situation, but the attorney can give you an educated guess.
- **Can you estimate a total cost for my case?** The attorney should be able to give you a ballpark figure. Don't be surprised if your case costs more than $10,000.
- **Will I receive a written contract for your services?** The contract may also be called a retainer agreement or a retainer letter. Make sure you work with an attorney who will provide one.
- **What expenses am I responsible for?** Find out what office expenses and court fees are not included in the hourly rate.
- **How often will I be billed?** Most attorneys will bill monthly.
- **Can a payment plan be worked out?** Some attorneys are willing to do this, so if you need a flexible payment schedule, keep looking until you find someone who offers it.

- **Will you be handling my case personally?** If not, ask to meet the person who will be, and make sure one person is in charge of your case. At some large firms, junior associates may take over a case.
- **How long do you estimate the case will take?** The attorney should be able to estimate when the process will be concluded.
- **Do you feel I have a good chance of getting what I want?** Try to get a feeling for how this person views your chances.
- **What am I asking for that I might not get?** This question will require the attorney to be specific. Even if the news is bad, it is important to know it now.

- **Do you plan on trying to settle this case?** Most lawyers will engage in settlement negotiations. Settlement is always cheaper than trial from your perspective.
- **How long does it take you to return phone calls?** You want a firm that will return calls within twenty-four hours.
- **Do you use e-mail for client communication?** This is often the fastest way to reach your attorney, but some still do not use e-mail due to privacy concerns.
- **Will I be able to track my case online?** Your state court may have a system you can log into, and your attorney's office may also have an internal system through which clients can check progress.
- **Who can I reach if there is a problem after hours?** It is rare to find an attorney who has a 24/7 emergency line, but it is still a good idea to ask.
- **Is someone available to handle emergencies if you are unavailable?** This can be a paralegal or another attorney.

Think about the answers you get and evaluate whether this is someone you feel comfortable with.

SHOULD YOU FILE YOUR OWN DIVORCE?

Because attorney bills can be expensive, you're probably wondering if you really need an attorney. It is possible to file for divorce on your own, but often it is not a good idea. An attorney can help you understand what you are entitled to, how a court would decide your case, and how to protect your rights. You can consider filing yourself if the following are true:

- You have no significant marital debts or assets to divide.
- There are no pensions or retirement funds to divide.
- You do not want alimony and your spouse is not asking for it.
- You have no children or completely agree about custody and child support.
- Domestic violence is not an issue.

Check your state court website for the forms needed to file "pro se" (on your own) or ask for them at the courthouse. Be aware that there are many deadlines and forms, and if you make a mistake or file anything late, it could completely change your rights.

28

Understanding What Your Attorney Needs from You

Your lawyer cannot manage your case without your help. Because divorces deal primarily with financial and custody matters, you need to provide your attorney with all the information he or she requests, including records of finances, expenses, debts, and property. Expect to be asked to divulge personal information, such as the reason for your divorce, financial status, and things that will support your custody position (information on your lifestyle and parenting abilities, as well as all the details about why you don't want your ex to have custody). You have all the facts in the case, and it is your job to convey them to your attorney accurately and in a form that is easy to access so he or she can input the information into court documents. This will make your case easier to prepare and present. The less time your attorney spends doing this, the less it will cost you, so it's in your best interest to put all of this information together as succinctly as possible.

Many clients are not completely honest with their divorce attorneys. They don't supply needed documents, or they leave out important pieces of information, especially anything that makes them look bad. You may feel uncomfortable about having to give out private information, but it is for your own benefit. Your attorney is there to help you. You are a team, so make sure you are honest with him or her.

Be a client who is calm, coherent, and reasonable. Lawyers spend a lot of time calming people down and listening to descriptions of personal feelings, even though they are not trained to do this. Your attorney will handle the legal aspect of your divorce, but he or she is not trained to help you cope with the emotional aspect. Therapists cost much less per hour than attorneys, so see one if you need to, instead of paying your attorney to listen.

Be a client who can follow instructions. When your attorney asks you to provide information, the information is necessary. If you don't understand a request, ask for clarification. Try to follow all of the requests and advice as best you can. You will save money if your attorney does not have to spend additional time helping you get the information together.

Let your lawyer know you have purchased this book, and give him or her copies of all the lists, logs, and documents you create. Take this book and your files (digital and/or paper) with you to every meeting you have with your attorney and to every court appearance. Keep them in a convenient place at home so that if you are on the phone with your attorney, you have the information at hand.

Do not share this book with your spouse! It will help you work on strategy and documentation. No matter how friendly your relationship is, you need to play some cards close to the vest.

Working with Your Lawyer

Working with an attorney takes some patience. You have to remember that he or she has other cases. While yours is important, others might be more pressing at certain times (just as there will be times when your case will be pressing and garner a lot of his or her attention). However, this doesn't mean that your questions or concerns should be ignored.

It's up to you to convey the seriousness of your concerns, but if you call twice a week with an "urgent" concern or e-mail every day, your attorney isn't going to be very quick to respond. It's important to be patient with him or her, but you also need to know when to stand up and say, "I need something right now"—a careful balancing act at times. You

AVOID TIME AND MONEY BUSTERS

Follow these tips to save time and money:

- Call only when you have something important to discuss. Don't call just for an update. When there's something to report, your attorney will tell you.
- If you are trying to decide how to handle something that relates to your case (such as refusing to allow your children to go on a set visitation, deciding whether you should turn an asset over to your spouse, or moving out of the home), check with your attorney *before* you do anything. It is much easier to have a five-minute phone call that resolves the problem than to have your lawyer try to undo damage after the fact.
- If your case is on an online tracking system you can access, check there before you call the law office to ask questions about progress.
- Present documents and papers in an orderly way. If you give your attorney a disorganized heap of papers, you're going to pay for someone in the office to straighten it out. If you send digital files that are not clearly marked and labeled, they will get lost in the shuffle.
- Keep copies of all documents and digital files in case your lawyer can't find something.
- Whenever possible, talk to a secretary or paralegal instead of the attorney. These other professionals bill at a lower hourly rate (or may not bill at all).
- When you meet with your lawyer, keep chitchat to a minimum. Remember, you are paying for his or her time.
- Try to work out informal agreements about custody, visitation, and property and debt division with your spouse on your own. Write down what you've agreed to and then ask your attorney to formalize these decisions for you with a court order. Anything you can decide on your own will drastically reduce your legal bills.
- Do not call the law office at every single bump in the road or exchange of words with your ex. Keep track of all the small issues, and if they are still problems, you can discuss them at your next meeting or during your next phone call.
- Work with a mediator to settle unresolved issues. Most mediators bill at a lower hourly rate than attorneys, and both you and your spouse receive services at that lower rate. See Chapter 6 and the section on other professionals in this chapter for more information about mediation.
- Don't go to an appointment if you haven't gathered the necessary documents or facts. Reschedule the meeting for a time when you will have the information at hand.
- Read a book or consult the Internet to answer your most general questions about divorce law in your state so you don't need to take up your attorney's time with explanations of the basics.
- Don't hide problems or important issues. They will almost always come back to bite you later, causing bigger problems and more legal bills than they would have if they had been dealt with up front. Be honest with your attorney, even if you aren't honest with anyone else.

don't want to involve your lawyer in every disagreement you have with your spouse or every conflict that occurs with visitation. You do, however, want to let him or her know when major crises develop. Don't be timid when you need advice or information. If you don't get a timely response from your attorney when you need something, call again and leave a detailed message, or send an e-mail marked Urgent. Another trick to keep in mind is that a fax can sometimes be a way to get immediate attention: it ends up on your attorney's desk and is hard to miss!

If your attorney has a legal secretary or paralegal, you can try to speak to him or her. Although these professionals generally are not able to give you advice, they may be able to reach the attorney to get an answer to your question or problem, or they may even be able to answer a question. Time is money when it comes to legal representation. The more time you spend with your attorney, the more it's going to cost you. That's why it is important to approach meetings or phone calls in an organized way. Think about your questions or issues in advance, and list them on the Questions and Issues to Discuss with Your Attorney worksheet at the end of this chapter. Take notes on everything your lawyer tells you, especially when on the phone; afterward, make notes about the answers to your questions. You may have a good memory, but there are so many emotional issues involved that you won't always be thinking clearly. If you take clear notes, you can return to them later to refresh your memory, to back up what the attorney has told you, or to clarify information you've provided.

It's almost impossible to ask all your questions in the first meeting. You will forget things, and new questions will arise after the meeting, which is to be expected. Remember one of the rules from Chapter 1: don't be too hard on yourself.

Save all e-mails from your attorney in a separate folder so you can access them easily to double-check things or follow up.

Organizing Documents from Your Attorney

In the course of your case, you will receive several kinds of documents from your attorney. Some will be informational, like pamphlets, information sheets, and statements of your rights. Others will require you to fill in information and return them (digitally or on paper). Still others will be copies of court papers and correspondence that you should keep in chronological order by issue date. If you receive forms via e-mail, move them to the divorce folder on your computer, labeling them appropriately. If you don't have time to fill them out immediately, put them on your to-do list so you don't forget. If you find it easier to read hard copy items, print them out. Store paper documents you need to fill in and return, as well as the ones you need to keep, in your accordion file.

Phone Calls and E-mails with Professionals

You'll probably have many phone calls with your attorney and the other professionals involved in your case. Use the Phone Call Log to keep notes about these calls. Write down appointments, instructions, and any other information you are given.

A phone call log can be helpful if you are having difficulty getting in touch with your attorney. Make a note each time you leave him or her a message. If you've left several messages with no response, you can call back and say, "I left messages on the twelfth, thirteenth, fourteenth, and fifteenth but have not heard back yet."

You should keep e-mails in a separate folder in your mail program so you can find them easily. You don't necessarily need to keep an e-mail log, since you can see when your last contact was, but if you will feel more organized (or are afraid you will lose e-mails), use the E-mail Log at the end of this chapter to do so.

Paying Your Attorney

You will receive bills from the law office, as well as receipts for retainer fees and court fees that you've paid up front. Like any other office, this office can make billing mistakes, so check your invoices for accuracy. Make sure you record payments you make in your checkbook; if you pay with cash or credit, always ask for a receipt.

While some attorneys are willing to make allowances for clients who don't pay on time, others may drop you as a client, charge you interest, or begin collection proceedings if you don't pay.

Affording Your Attorney

Make sure you know up front how much your divorce is going to cost you. Get a clear estimate during your initial consultation. Ask your attorney if he or she will agree to payment plans (some firms use special financing companies that allow you to spread payments out, but there are fees involved). You'll find that your monthly legal bill will be small in the beginning, but once you are in the trial phase of your case, it can be quite large. Costs will be more manageable if they can be spread into equal payments over several months.

If you don't have the funds to pay your legal bills, think about borrowing money from family or friends. This is one of those times when you have to call in favors. Many divorce clients end up paying their legal bills this way. If you have a low income and few assets, contact a legal aid clinic to find out if you qualify for free or reduced-fee legal assistance. Your local bar association can give you the number.

If your spouse has a higher income than you do, the court may direct him or her to pay your legal bills. Talk to your attorney about this possibility at your initial meeting.

Legal bills are going to be a major expense you must face, but remember that paying them will move your divorce forward.

Other Professionals Who May Be Involved with Your Case

Your attorney is probably the most important professional you will be dealing with throughout the divorce process, but other people also may become involved in your case.

32

Keep a detailed contact list so you can contact these people easily when you need them. Use the Master List of Contact Information at the end of this chapter to record their phone numbers and e-mail addresses. Storing these names and numbers in your phone is important, but it's also a good idea to have a separate list because, frankly, a month from now you may not remember the name of the appraiser your attorney has called in.

Law Guardian/Guardian ad Litem

The court may appoint a law guardian, or guardian *ad litem*, to represent your child or children in the custody part of the case. This is an attorney who represents the children's point of view about custody and visitation. Law guardians are often paid by the state, but in some instances, the parents are required to pay the fees.

These attorneys are specially trained and are skilled at meeting children and understanding custody issues. The law guardian will probably contact you at the beginning of the case and may ask to set up a home visit or ask you and your child to go to his or her office. During the visit, he or she will talk with you about your relationship with your child and your point of view about custody. He or she may also ask to speak privately with your child.

While it is a good idea to ask your attorney how to deal with the law guardian, it is usually in your best interest to be friendly and cooperative. In some states, the law guardian makes a recommendation to the judge about custody and is very influential. You want him or her to be sympathetic to your view. Remember, however, that this person is not necessarily on your side, so don't spill your guts. Be a little calculating in your dealings with the law guardian: be honest and friendly, but keep in mind that this person is really there to judge you. You want to put your best foot forward in all of your dealings with the law guardian.

Keep any written correspondence from the law guardian in the accordion folder and keep a digital folder for his or her e-mails as well.

Appraiser

You may need to hire an appraiser to value your home, business, or other assets. Appraisers provide an estimated value of an asset so the court has a number to work from when creating a property settlement. Be sure to select one who has experience with the type of asset(s) you need valued. Your attorney will hire the appraiser but may ask for your input. Since you're paying, you can say you want the right of approval over who is chosen. In some cases, both spouses may hire appraisers, and the court may request a third.

It is usually in your best interest to help the appraiser reach an accurate valuation. If the asset you are given is not really worth what it is appraised at, you have lost out on tangible value. For example, suppose you are awarded an RV that is appraised at $50,000, while your spouse is given investments worth $50,000. Unfortunately, you can't get anyone to buy the RV for $50,000 because it is really worth only $30,000. That means you've just lost $20,000. Conversely, if an appraiser undervalues an asset and it goes to your spouse, your spouse ends up with a higher value than the court intended.

Keep all copies of reports and bills from appraisers in your accordion or digital file.

Counselor/Therapist and Evaluator

A large number of families participate in counseling as part of the divorce process. Counseling can be helpful for you and your child, because counselors can suggest coping mechanisms for the rocky times of a divorce. They offer a place for you and your child to talk freely without fear of repercussion. Some divorcing couples attend counseling together to learn how to coparent and make their split less acrimonious.

Here are ways to find a counselor:

- Ask your family doctor or pediatrician for a referral.
- Check the list of counselors who participate in your insurance plan.
- Ask family and friends for the names of counselors they've used.

Check out a counselor's website and Google the name to see other people's opinions and to learn about his or her qualifications. Once you've found a counselor, you'll want to ask him or her the following questions:

- How experienced are you with children?
- How long have you been in practice?
- How experienced are you with issues of divorce?
- How much will the sessions cost?
- Do you participate in my insurance plan?
- Are you available by phone if emergencies come up?
- What is the hourly rate?
- How quickly can we/I get an appointment?

In the course of a custody case, you may be required to see a counselor, therapist, or psychologist for a parenting evaluation. This professional is not there to help you work through problems but to provide the court with an opinion about each parent's abilities and the family dynamics. You won't gain anything by being uncooperative in these situations, so be honest when possible. Talk with your attorney if you are concerned about how to approach these evaluations.

Mental health evaluations are another situation, in which the court has a professional evaluate your mental health, usually to determine if you are able to parent appropriately or pose any danger to your child. If you are referred for one of these evaluations, it is easy to feel resentful when you are certain there is nothing wrong with you. Talk with your attorney about what to expect and approach this as just another step in your divorce process.

Caseworker

If an allegation of child abuse is made, state child and family services or social services caseworkers may be called in to investigate the allegations. If an investigation is initiated, notify your lawyer as soon as you know about it. Keep any pertinent documents in the accordion file and share them with your attorney. Treat caseworkers politely and respectfully.

Financial Adviser

If you have a financial adviser, you may need to contact him or her to obtain documents about your investments. Once you are divorced, it is a good idea to see separate financial planners to avoid any conflict or mistrust.

Accountant or Divorce Planner

Some attorneys routinely use accountants to assist them in planning a divorce settlement. If your case involves a closely held business or other complicated finances, an accountant can help untangle all the information. A certified divorce planner is a specially trained financial expert brought in by your attorney who will help you reach a settlement and explain the ramifications of financial decisions during divorce.

When working with an accountant or divorce planner, you need to consider your financial position. If you own a business and want the value minimized, you won't be as forthcoming with information as you would be if you were the nonowner spouse. Discuss the possibilities with your attorney.

Retain all documents and bills from these financial professionals.

Mediator

A mediator is a neutral party who helps a divorcing couple reach a mutually acceptable settlement. Some states require that divorcing couples try mediation before heading to court. A mediator does not represent either you or your spouse but works for both of you. You and your spouse need to have separate attorneys during mediation to explain what your legal rights are. The attorneys also approve the settlement that is reached in mediation and then take it to court to finalize it. To make mediation work, you must approach it with a willing attitude and some faith in the process. Sometimes a mediator can help you resolve the issues involved in your divorce more quickly than an attorney can.

If you are referred to mediation by the court, you are required to try it, but you are not required to reach an agreement there. It is to your benefit to try to reach a resolution in mediation, because it will save you thousands of dollars in legal fees.

Collaborative Lawyers

Collaborative lawyers work with the spouses and each other to reach a settlement; the process is similar to mediation, but the attorneys do most of the talking. If you work with a collaborative lawyer and do not reach a settlement, you need to seek a new attorney to take your case to court, since collaborative lawyers do not try cases.

QUESTIONS AND ISSUES TO DISCUSS WITH YOUR ATTORNEY

Print copies of this list for further use.

Date _____

Questions

_____
_____
_____
_____
_____
_____
_____
_____
_____
_____
_____
_____

Notes

_____
_____
_____
_____
_____
_____
_____
_____
_____
_____
_____
_____

PHONE CALL LOG

Print copies of this log for further use.

Person	Date	Time	Notes

MASTER LIST OF CONTACT INFORMATION

Print copies of this log for further use.

Name	Address	Business Phone	Cell Phone	E-mail Address

E-MAIL LOG

Print copies of this log for further use.

Person	Date	Time	Notes

4

Ways to End Your Marriage

While ending a marriage is never easy, you do have some choices to consider about the way you end your relationship. Divorce, separation, and annulment are options to talk to your attorney about.

Divorce

If you are reading this book, you are likely considering or have begun a divorce. There are certain requirements involved.

Residency

Before you can file for divorce, you must meet your state's *residency requirements*. These are laws requiring you and/or your spouse to live in that state for a certain period of time before filing for divorce. The time frame can range from a few weeks to a year. To find your state requirements, check your state court website, or see the information provided by the American Bar Association at http://www.americanbar.org/groups/family_law /resources/family_law_in_the_50_states.html.

Grounds

The *grounds for divorce* is the legal reason why the marriage is being dissolved. All states have no-fault divorce options that allow you to ask for a divorce without placing blame on either party. You can indicate that you have irreconcilable differences, are incompatible, or have had an irretrievable breakdown in the relationship. Neither spouse needs to prove that this is true, and no evidence is presented to the court. Your spouse can still contest the divorce, but it is rare for a divorce to be denied in this situation. Some states will permit no-fault divorces only after you've been legally separated for a certain length of time, so be sure to talk to your attorney about the rules in your state.

You also have the option of providing an actual reason (called the grounds) for why you want a divorce. These reasons can include the following:

- **Abandonment.** Your spouse has left you or failed to support you.
- **Adultery.** Your spouse has had sexual intercourse with someone else during the marriage.
- **Cruel treatment.** Your spouse has treated you in a way that is mean or cruel (sometimes called cruel and inhuman, or cruel and inhumane, treatment).
- **Imprisonment.** Your spouse has been in prison during a portion of the marriage (there is normally a fixed minimum number of years to qualify) and must still be in prison when you file for the divorce.
- **Physical inability to have intercourse.** This ground can normally be used only if your spouse did not share this information with you prior to the marriage.

WHAT IS AN UNCONTESTED DIVORCE?

An uncontested divorce happens where one person (the plaintiff) files for divorce and the other spouse (defendant) either never responds or agrees to everything the plaintiff has asked for. This is the fastest and simplest way to get a divorce.

All of the grounds used by the plaintiff (the spouse requesting the divorce) relate to what the defendant (the other spouse) has done during the marriage. For example, you can't ask for a divorce because *you've* cheated on your spouse; you can only ask for a divorce because your spouse has cheated on *you*. A defendant can file a counterclaim asking the court to end the marriage because of something the plaintiff did. It's important to consult an attorney, because laws about grounds vary greatly, and you must meet the exact requirements set out in your state law.

You will also want to discuss the fastest and least expensive grounds for your case. While you might feel better if you can prove to the world that your spouse is an adulterer, it ultimately may not make sense to pursue this as your grounds due to the expense involved.

Often, a couple agrees on the grounds, and the defendant legally consents to them. If there is no contest over the grounds, the plaintiff usually gives a short statement to the court about the facts that support the grounds, but there is no cross-examination, testimony from witnesses, or presentation of evidence.

Although it is rare to have a grounds trial, it does happen occasionally. This means that the plaintiff has given a reason for the divorce, and the defendant does not agree that he or she has done anything wrong and does not agree that there should be a divorce. Should this happen in your case, you will have a hearing just about the grounds. Your attorney will present evidence and testimony, and your spouse's attorney will have the opportunity to cross-examine and present evidence and testimony to refute your case. The judge will decide whether or not there are adequate grounds to dissolve the marriage. Note that it is possible to have a jury decide the grounds portion of your trial, although this rarely happens.

If you have to gather evidence for a grounds trial, try to collect the following:

Abandonment
- The date your spouse left
- Proof that your spouse has taken a new residence, such as mail that has been delivered there or your spouse listing the new address on documents or providing this as his or her correct address when asked
- Your recollections of conversations in which your spouse said he or she was leaving or of conversations in which he or she refused your requests for financial support
- Testimony from others about your spouse's intentions to leave
- Notes or journal entries you made around the time your spouse left

Imprisonment
- Information about your spouse's conviction and sentence (Case numbers and inmate numbers are helpful if you have them.)

Cruelty
- A list of everything you can recall that your spouse has done or said to you within the past two years that was cruel, painful, or dangerous (mentally, emotionally, or physically)
- Names of others who have witnessed your spouse's behavior
- Photographs and/or police reports documenting physical abuse by your spouse

Adultery
- Testimony from private investigators or others who have witnessed the adultery firsthand
- Photographs or video of the adultery

Physical Inability
- Notes of attempts to consummate the marriage and the outcomes
- Names of doctors who have been consulted

43

Annulment

An *annulment* is a legal decision by a court that the marriage was invalid at the time it occurred. Contrary to popular belief, it doesn't mean the marriage never happened; instead, it says the marriage was never legally valid. Any children born during the marriage are legally legitimate. A legal annulment is different from a religious annulment, which must be granted by a religious institution (for example, a Jewish annulment is called a get) and has its own criteria and process (consult your clergy member for information).

The following are some grounds for a legal annulment:

- Being underage at the time of the marriage
- Misrepresenting yourself (saying, for example, that you are able to have children when you know you can't)
- Being mentally ill
- Being unable or unwilling to consummate the marriage (have intercourse)
- Concealing important facts such as alcoholism or previous children

The criteria for annulments can vary greatly from state to state, so be sure to discuss this option with your attorney if it is something you're interested in. Since most annulments are sought soon after the wedding, there is usually no need to divide property, decide custody, or award support or alimony. However, if your annulment does occur after a longer marriage, these issues will be decided by the court as part of the annulment process.

Legal Separation

A *legal separation* is a court order stating that you and your spouse are to live separate and apart, but you remain married. These orders usually specify everything else that a divorce judgment contains, such as child support, alimony, and property division, but they do not formally dissolve the marriage. In some states, you can get a legal separation without going to court simply by having both spouses sign a separation agreement created by an attorney. The most common reason for seeking a separation is that some states require a certain period of legal separation before filing for a no-fault divorce.

Don't confuse a legal separation with physical separation. When you and your spouse move to separate residences, you have physically separated, but you have not obtained a legal separation until you sign a document or the court issues an order declaring you separated.

Remaining Married Without Separation Documentation

44

Some couples physically separate but never seek a legal separation or divorce. You are not required to divorce if you no longer want to live together—you can physically separate and go on with your lives. You will need to continue listing your married status on income tax returns and other legal documents. Child support and custody can be determined by your state's family court. It is also possible to obtain spousal support. Complications arise if you have trouble dividing your assets and debts on your own. Some people are able to do this themselves, whereas others need to take the matter to court. It's important to note that if you never divorce, your spouse is entitled to inherit a portion of your estate if you die before him or her, and you will also have similar rights to each other's Social Security benefits. Talk to your attorney if you are considering separating but remaining legally married.

Ending a Common-Law Marriage

In nine states (Alabama, Colorado, Iowa, Kansas, Montana, Rhode Island, South Carolina, Texas, and Utah) and Washington, DC, if you live together and hold yourselves out as a married couple (by introducing each other as "my husband" or "my wife," filing a joint tax return, or using the title Mrs., for example), your relationship becomes a legal marriage after a significant period of time—usually several years. If you meet the requirements of a common-law marriage in your state, then you will use your state's regular divorce procedure to end your marriage. If you do not meet these requirements, or if your state does not recognize common-law marriages, then you are not legally married, and divorce is not available to you. You can just physically separate. Custody and child support issues can be handled by your state's family court, but you will have to handle property and debt division on your own or in small-claims court. Talk to your attorney about this. Mediation can be the best way to handle the dissolution of a long-term relationship that is not a marriage.

Ending a Same-Sex Marriage

If you and your spouse are of the same sex and have been legally married in your state, you will follow the same divorce (or annulment or separation) process as other couples in your state. If you were legally married in a state other than the one you live in (and the one you live in does not recognize same-sex marriages), you can obtain a divorce in the state you were married in if you can meet the residency requirements set out by that state. You cannot obtain a divorce in your home state unless the law there changes to recognize same-sex marriage. You can determine custody and child support in family court in your home state whether you are legally married there or not, as long as you are both legal parents of the children. If you and your spouse cannot divorce in your state and cannot meet requirements to obtain a divorce in another state, you will need to work out the property distribution on your own or with a mediator.

5

Step-by-Step Through Your Divorce

The divorce process and the entire court system can appear intimidating, but they don't have to be. There is an order to the way things will progress in your case. Understanding this and what to expect will make the entire process easier, and you will find you have fewer questions for your attorney.

The System and the Way It Works

Because the court system is so foreign and the documents are usually written in confusing language, it's easy to feel as if you are in over your head. Once you understand what the court papers mean and how your case is going to proceed, you'll feel more organized and in control.

Initial Papers

Your divorce will begin with a petition, summons, or application for divorce (your state may use a different name) filed by the plaintiff, the spouse who is bringing the case to court. The petition lists what the plaintiff is asking for (such as custody, alimony, child support, and property and debt distribution) and either explains the grounds for the divorce or indicates that a no-fault divorce is being sought. This document has to be served on the other party, meaning given to them in a way that meets your state's requirements. This is often done by a process server. If you're the plaintiff, you will go over this with your attorney prior to filing.

If you're not the plaintiff (meaning you're the defendant) and you're served with this kind of document, keep it in a safe place because your attorney will need it. Store all of your court documents in your accordion folder or, if you receive an electronic copy, in the

E-FILING

In some states, divorce papers may be filed online. This means that instead of your attorney submitting hard copy forms to the court, documents are submitted electronically. Hard copy forms may still be given to you. It is to your benefit to consent to your attorney e-filing your case, as it reduces time and costs. (In some states, court fees are reduced for e-filing, so your attorney's costs will also be decreased. Your attorney may also be able to serve documents electronically, thereby reducing process server fees.) You may be able to initiate a divorce yourself on your state court site, but if you do so, be sure to note the case name and any passwords you set up so your attorney can access the case. If your lawyer does manage your case with e-filing, you can ask to have access to some of the documents online.

appropriate folder on your computer. If you are served with this kind of document it is very important that you talk to an attorney as soon as possible, because there is a short time limit on your opportunity to respond. If you do not respond, the case will move forward without you.

After the petition has been filed, the defendant has a chance to respond by filing a document called an appearance, a response, or an answer. Then the plaintiff will likely file more papers that give additional details about the divorce. These papers may be served by a process server, but if your attorney is in contact with your spouse's attorney, they will often handle the service.

Initial Court Appearance

A date will be set for an initial appearance, and both parties in the case must come to court. Your attorney will send you a copy of the notice or call you with the information. Make sure you keep the notice and record the date on your calendar, because it is mandatory that you appear. The initial appearance may occur soon after the initial papers are filed if one of the parties is asking the court for a temporary order. A *temporary order* is a preliminary court order that decides certain issues on a temporary basis, such as where the children will live, whether child support will be paid, and who will remain in the marital residence while the case is pending. A short hearing may be held to decide about temporary orders.

If there are no requests for temporary orders, the initial appearance is usually a settlement conference, where the lawyers meet with someone from the judge's staff and try to reach a settlement. There may be several such pretrial conferences, and the court may suggest mediation as an alternative.

Discovery

The next stage of the process is discovery, when each side gathers information in preparation for the trial. You may have to produce documents or answer written questions (with the assistance of your lawyer). In hotly contested cases, depositions are sometimes taken. A *deposition* is sworn testimony that is given in an attorney's office and transcribed by a stenographer. The attorney uses this opportunity to ask the opposing party questions that will help the attorney plan for the trial. If a deposition will be needed in your case, your attorney will help you prepare. Depositions sound like a duplication of the trial, but often they are a useful way to reach a settlement.

Settlement Meetings

Throughout the process, your attorney will be working to try to settle your case. He or she will speak with your spouse's attorney, and there will be a meeting with all attorneys and spouses. If a settlement is close, another settlement conference may be held at the courthouse.

Trial

MEDIATION PROCESS

If you are using mediation, you will complete all the initial divorce paperwork, then there will be a pause in trial preparation while you and your spouse meet with a mediator to try to reach a settlement. Nothing that is discussed in mediation is binding until you actually sign an agreement. Mediation is usually the fastest and least expensive way to conclude your case. If you reach an agreement in mediation, it will be written, approved by both attorneys, and signed. One attorney will then file the agreement with the court, and it will become the divorce decree.

If you do not reach a settlement, a trial will be scheduled. (Note, however, that most cases do settle rather than go to trial, although settlement may not happen until moments before the scheduled trial.) The trial is not usually completed in one day; it may be held in bits and pieces over several days.

When a trial is held, each side gives an *opening statement*, or brief summary of the case. Afterward, the plaintiff's attorney calls witnesses and presents evidence. The defendant has a chance to cross-examine those witnesses. Then the defendant presents witnesses and evidence, and the plaintiff can cross-examine. The trial ends with *closing statements* in which each attorney states what he or she is asking for and how he or she wants the judge to rule.

The divorce will not be final until the judge's decision is rendered in writing. Most judges won't tell you what they've decided while you are in court. They make their decisions only in writing, and that can take several weeks. Once you get the decision, your attorney may have some paperwork to complete to finalize the divorce.

Appeals

An appeal asks a higher, more powerful court to review the decision made by the trial court. An appellate court reviews only issues of law, not issues of fact. This means that it decides only whether or not the trial court applied the law properly in the case. The appellate court does not hear any new evidence or testimony, and there are no witnesses. It is purely a review of the legal decision made by the trial judge.

Appeals are most common at the end of the case—after the judge has issued a final ruling. However, your attorney can appeal temporary, initial, and interim orders and decisions at any point in the case.

If you feel that the decision made in your case is wrong or unfair, discuss it with your attorney. You have only a certain period of time in which to begin an appeal, and if you miss the window, there's nothing you can do.

If you decide to appeal, understand that it can be a lengthy (and expensive) process. You will not need to appear at any time. Your attorney will prepare a written *brief*, or argument, and send it to the appellate court. Your attorney may also appear in court to give an oral argument. Because the brief focuses completely on how the law was applied in your case, there is nothing you can do to assist your attorney in preparing it.

Court Papers

Throughout your divorce, your attorney will collect numerous documents about your case, and you will receive copies of many of them. Keep them in a separate file with the most recent documents at the front. If your attorney e-mails you digital copies, keep them organized in a file on your computer. Then, if you need to double-check on a court date, you can easily find the most recent notice.

Your attorney will prepare all the documents to file in your case, and you will be required to sign them (physically or electronically) and swear they are true. Because of this, it is important that you take the time to read them and make sure they are accurate before signing them. Double-check numbers on financial statements if they don't look right to you, and make sure the papers ask for everything you want. It is much harder to change things after they have been filed, so you want the papers to be accurate. Do not assume your attorney has gotten everything right!

Your attorney will also give you copies of documents filed by your spouse. Read them carefully and point out things that are not true or that you disagree with. It can be helpful to make a list to give to your attorney. (Use the Response to Divorce Papers from Spouse form at the end of this chapter.) Remember to save venting for friends and family. Use your time with your attorney to get down to business.

Here are some terms you may encounter when dealing with court papers:

Affiant. The person signing an affidavit
Affidavit. A sworn written statement
Allegations. Things a person claims to be true
Amend. To change a court paper
Answer. A paper filed by a defendant in response to the plaintiff's papers
Complaint. A form that lists specific reasons for divorce
Default. To not appear in court or to fail to respond to court papers
Docket number. Case number
Ex parte. Without the other party present (Sometimes a judge will make an emergency decision with only one party in the courtroom.)
Jurisdiction. A court's ability to hear certain cases
Litigants. Parties involved in the case (plaintiff and defendant)
Motion. A formal way of asking the court to decide something
Notary. A licensed official who verifies signatures on papers

50

Pleadings. Initial court papers
Pro se. Without an attorney
Stipulation. An agreement or settlement

Most legal papers are sprinkled with legalese—words like *witnesseth, hereby, adjudged, decreed, therefore, in accordance with, pursuant,* and so on. These words are often just formalities without much meaning. Don't get bogged down by the language. You don't need to know the exact definition of every word; you just need a sense of what the document says. If there is something substantial you don't understand, ask your attorney. To save money, if your attorney has a paralegal working on your case, ask him or her instead of your attorney (paralegals bill at a lower hourly rate).

MILITARY DIVORCE

Military divorces are governed by state laws like other divorces, but federal laws also apply. A military person cannot be sued for divorce while on active duty. Jurisdiction for a military divorce is decided based on where the service person holds legal residence, not where he or she actually is while in service. Residency rules are also often altered for military personnel. To serve a member of the military, you must get permission from the military to do so. Your attorney can explain these rules in more detail.

Appearing in Court

Going to court to have your divorce decided can be a momentous and stressful occasion. Most people have only been in court for things like traffic tickets or jury duty. If you know what to expect in advance and arrive prepared, you can go to court feeling, if not confident, at least organized and knowledgeable. Remember that very few people other than lawyers feel completely at ease in court. Judges and court personnel understand how you feel and often go out of their way to make you comfortable.

How to Dress

People are often judged by their appearance. When you go to court, it is important that you dress neatly and seriously. Avoid clothes and accessories that look flashy or too casual, including the following:

- Hats
- Open-toed shoes
- Sandals, slides, or flip-flops
- A lot of jewelry, no matter how tasteful
- Large jewelry (real or fake)
- Loud or flashy clothing
- Ripped or torn clothing
- Big or messy hair (make sure most of your face is uncovered)
- Messy facial stubble or unkempt facial hair
- T-shirts, tank tops, or tops with spaghetti straps

- Shorts
- Jeans
- Tight, see-through, or revealing clothing
- Many exposed tattoos
- Excessive makeup
- Very long or flashy fingernails
- Wrinkled or stained clothing
- Sunglasses
- Work boots
- Body or facial piercings (other than ears)
- Very short skirts
- Sneakers
- Stiletto heels

The preferred attire for men is a sport coat and tie or a dress shirt and tie. A sweater or a shirt with a collar is also appropriate. For women it's a suit, dress, skirt, or dress pants. When deciding what to wear, keep in mind that this is how you want to look:

- Respectable
- Serious
- Conservative
- Responsible
- Reliable
- Trustworthy
- Dependable
- Financially modest
- Friendly

Certainly you are who you are, but when you go to court, you aren't there to make a political or fashion statement. You're there to win over the judge and get what you want. This means you've got to play by the judge's rules. Judges like litigants who dress conservatively, act appropriately, and look like upstanding citizens. Dress the part.

Since you will probably have to go to court several times, assemble a few outfits in advance to choose from. This way you won't panic the morning of your hearing. Always have a backup outfit in case something is wrong with the one you choose.

Understanding Courtroom Procedures

Everyone has seen courtrooms—either on reality TV or on drama shows. For the most part, real courtrooms are similar to the TV versions, except there is much less drama!

The Courtroom
Some courtrooms are huge, formal places. Others are small, plain rooms, sometimes in temporary buildings or annexes. Ask your attorney where your courtroom is and how to get there. Ask what kind of room it is and where you should meet.

The judge will sit behind a bench or desk that may be raised or at eye level. There will usually be at least two or three tables for the parties and their attorneys. Generally, the plaintiff sits on the right and the defendant on the left, but this can vary according to local custom or the judge. Sit where your attorney tells you.

Many courtrooms are open to the public, which means that people (including the media) can come in and observe. Unless your case is high profile, it is unlikely that anyone will observe your proceedings. If this is something you're worried about, talk to your attorney. It is possible to have the details of your case closed to the public.

Court Personnel

When you enter the courthouse, you will probably first encounter security personnel. They will ask you to step through a metal detector and may x-ray or search your belongings. Note that weapons and sharp objects are not permitted in courthouses. If you aren't certain about the rules, call the courthouse in advance to check, or ask your attorney.

You may next encounter a court clerk. If there is a waiting room, you will need to check in and let the clerk know you're there. A bailiff usually calls the cases. Bailiffs generally wear uniforms and keep order in the courtroom.

Inside the courtroom, there may be a court stenographer who transcribes everything that is said during the proceedings. Some cases are tape-recorded rather than transcribed. There may also be a court clerk or secretary inside the courtroom to assist the judge with scheduling and paperwork.

When you go to court initially, you may not appear in front of a judge. Instead, you may meet with a matrimonial referee, law clerk, hearing officer, or some other quasi-judicial person. Ask your lawyer in advance who is presiding. Whoever presides over your case is acting in an official capacity and must be treated with respect. Judges should be referred to as "Your Honor." Other personnel can be referred to as "Sir" or "Ma'am."

Courtroom Manners

If you're represented by an attorney, you shouldn't need to do a lot of talking in the courtroom. In general, you should talk only when the situation calls for it:

- The judge directly asks you a question.
- Your lawyer asks you a question.
- You have something urgent or important you need to tell your attorney (and then you should whisper it, not speak out in court).
- You are on the witness stand.

Don't talk to your spouse or your spouse's attorney while in the courtroom (unless the attorney is questioning you), and never interrupt when the judge is speaking.

When you are in the courtroom, you must stand whenever the judge does so (usually when he or she is entering or exiting). You will be asked to stand when the judge is making a decision or issuing an order. Your attorney will let you know what to do if you are unsure.

You must be certain your cell phone is turned off completely during the proceedings. Some judges become very angry if the proceedings are interrupted. You should not even look at your phone while in the courtroom, and texting or talking on the phone is a big mistake. Don't even put your phone on the table unless you absolutely need it to consult documents you have stored on it.

Do not chew gum or tobacco or eat candy or any food item during courtroom proceedings. A water bottle might be permitted on the table—ask your attorney; otherwise, keep it in your bag or on the floor.

Do not bring your children to court! They should never appear there unless your attorney specifically asks you to bring them.

What to Bring to Court

You can rely on your attorney to handle the paperwork involved in your divorce, but no one is infallible. Thus, it's always best to be prepared. Assume your attorney will have everything, but take all of your documents along just in case. That includes financial affidavits and statements, pay stubs, your calendar, and temporary or previous court orders. Take the forms from this book and your accordion or digital files with you. If you have remained organized, you will have everything you could possibly need at your fingertips. It is also a good idea to take along a notepad and pen in case you want to write your attorney a note in court or jot down things to ask about later. If your documents are on your laptop or tablet, you may take this into the courtroom, but you should not open it or turn it on unless your attorney tells you to.

Find out in advance how long you can expect to be at court. If it is an all-day trial, do a little research before you go to find a place nearby for lunch, or you can pack something to eat during the lunch break. You may be able to eat in the waiting room or in the lobby of the courthouse. Your attorney may have lunch with you, or he or she may need to go back to the office during the break. Do not openly take food, beverages, or gum into the courtroom. (If you packed a lunch, keep it out of sight in your bag.) Most large courthouses have food vendors or vending machines you can use during breaks.

Some people like to take along a friend or relative for support. If you do, he or she will not sit at your table in the courtroom and may even be asked to wait in the hall. Do not turn to look at or talk to your companion during court proceedings.

What Can Happen in Court

What can happen in court depends on what you are scheduled for. Initial appearances can include arguments about temporary orders as well as short hearings (where you may need to testify) to determine how the judge will rule on temporary requests. A judge can issue new or altered temporary orders at any appearance.

Once the temporary orders are in place, court appearances are usually for settlement purposes. The attorneys generally meet in private with court personnel to discuss possible settlements. Your attorney may come out to talk over possible compromises with you and then go back into the meeting.

When you go to court for hearings and trial, the atmosphere will be more formal and procedural. The plaintiff calls witnesses, and the defense gets to cross-examine them.

Once the plaintiff has called all witnesses and presented all of his or her documentary evidence, the defense presents its case, and the plaintiff cross-examines defense witnesses. In many states, if custody is an issue, a law guardian or guardian *ad litem* is appointed to represent the children. The law guardian can cross-examine all witnesses called in the custody phase of the trial and can present his or her own witnesses as well.

The Unexpected

If something is said in court that is not true and you believe your attorney is not aware of it, make a point of letting him or her know. If he or she has some facts or dates wrong, don't be afraid to point it out, but do so quietly by whispering or writing.

If you become overwrought with anger or sadness, ask your attorney to request a break to get yourself together. Everyone involved in the case understands how emotional it is. Take a walk outside to calm down and come back ready to get through the rest of the proceedings. You can also always ask for a bathroom break should one be needed. Most judges have several breaks throughout a trial.

Avoid any direct conflict with your spouse. At this point, you really have nothing you need to say to each other. Your attorneys will probably make sure this doesn't happen, but if your spouse tries to start an argument with you in the hall or waiting room, move away. If that doesn't help, call for security. If you get to court and your attorney isn't there, don't panic. Attorneys often have other cases scheduled at the same time. If your case is called and he or she has not yet appeared, let the bailiff or court clerk know. The court will either call the attorney or postpone the appearance. It's also OK for you to call your attorney's cell if you have it. His or her office may also know where he or she is. Do not proceed without your attorney. Note that if your attorney is consistently late or frequently misses court appearances, you may need to discuss the problem with him or her.

TAKE THE TIME YOU NEED

I often hear from people who went to court for a settlement conference and suddenly found themselves signing a settlement or agreeing to one on the record. It is not uncommon to go to court thinking it is just a routine appearance where nothing much will happen and having it become the finale to your case. If you need time to think about a settlement, say so. Don't let yourself be pushed into signing or agreeing to something you are going to regret down the road. It took a long time to decide to file for divorce. You should feel free to take as much time as you need to think about the settlement. The attorneys do want to wrap the case up, but what is more important is being certain about making such a final decision. If you don't feel ready to decide that day, it's OK to say so and ask for some time to think it over. Be aware that gives your spouse time to think as well and what seemed like a mutually acceptable agreement may fall apart if one or the other of you decides not to go forward.

RESPONSE TO DIVORCE PAPERS FROM SPOUSE

The following items listed in my spouse's papers are untrue:

_____

_____

_____

_____

_____

_____

_____

_____

_____

_____

_____

I do not agree with the following items my spouse is asking for:

_____

_____

_____

_____

_____

_____

_____

_____

_____

_____

_____

6

Settlement Options

Most divorcing couples end up settling. A settlement is usually the most desirable way to end a divorce, since both parties walk away feeling that they have won in some way. It also avoids the need for hurtful testimony and expensive trials. A trial often causes people to say or do things that are hard to forget or forgive. It pits you directly against each other in a way that makes it difficult to ever work together as parents. A settlement allows you to work out an agreement that is best for both of you (and your children) without having to testify against each other. Although judges try to make decisions that are fair, they don't know your situation as well as you do and can't possibly understand everything involved. Creating a settlement gives you control over the situation and allows you to tailor an agreement to your needs. Settlements are particularly preferred when it comes to custody and visitation. There are several paths you can take to get to a settlement.

Mediation

Mediation is a process in which both parties in the divorce meet with a mediator who acts as a neutral third party. The mediator helps explore the settlement options and encourages the divorcing couple to create a settlement that fits their personal needs. The mediator works for both spouses, remaining completely neutral. He or she does not make decisions for the couple but helps them find the solutions themselves.

In some states, mediation is mandatory—you have to try it before you can continue through the court process. In most states, though, it is still a relatively untraveled path.

The Benefits of Mediation

Mediation offers many benefits. The process teaches conflict-resolution skills, so the parties emerge with new methods to help them resolve problems that may arise in the future with regard to parental access or finances.

Additionally, mediation allows couples to take charge of their situation. Going to court and having a judge decide your fate can be a passive and frustrating experience. By engaging in mediation, you take the reins and actively search for solutions; the mediator is there as a guide and a resource but does not make any decisions. The solutions found in mediation are customized to fit each couple's particular needs and are far more detailed than the orders most courts would issue. And because they help create the settlements, couples are more likely to abide by them.

Mediated settlements provide closure in ways court decisions can't. You and your spouse work through a defined process that is very personal, and together you create an agreement that resolves your problems; you do all of this by working with each other and compromising. In most cases, participants walk away feeling satisfied and relieved. Mediation ends up being much less expensive than a contested divorce and allows the couple to avoid a lot of the anger that accompanies a traditional divorce. The focus is on solutions, not problems.

Mediation also is a great benefit for the children in a divorce. Instead of having their parents at each other's throats, dragging each other into court and using their children as weapons, the parents work together to decide how they will parent in the future. This creates a cooperative atmosphere that truly benefits the children. Some mediators even invite older children into the sessions so their opinions are heard. Mediation provides a good conflict-resolution model for kids. They see that the best way to solve problems is by talking about them and compromising.

Deciding Whether Mediation Is for You

To decide if mediation is right for you, ask yourself these questions:

- Am I fearful for my physical safety?
- Has domestic violence or spousal abuse ever been an issue in my marriage?
- Am I intimidated by my spouse?
- Does my spouse refuse to listen to me?
- Do I have a hard time standing up for what I want?
- Am I uncomfortable sitting in the same room with my spouse?
- Is my spouse unwilling to try to compromise?
- Would I be happier having an attorney handle all decisions for me?
- Do I have trouble expressing what I want or talking about the divorce without getting upset?
- Am I really just out for revenge?

If you answered yes to some of these questions, mediation may not work for you. If you are unsure, talk to your attorney.

Choosing a Mediator

If you think mediation is something you and your spouse should at least consider, set up an appointment for a free consultation with a local mediator. If you already have a matrimonial attorney, ask him or her for a referral to a mediator. Some attorneys are resistant to mediation because they see it as taking work away from them, but a matrimonial attorney should be in favor of anything that reduces conflict and benefits the client. Don't let your attorney talk you out of mediation if it is something you would like to try.

To find a mediator, you can also contact your local bar association's referral program or check the list of resources at the end of this book. Many states have mediation associations that can refer you to a mediator in your area.

The mediator will want to meet with you and your spouse together. Since he or she must remain neutral, meeting with either of you alone would be unethical. The mediator works for both of you.

Most states don't license mediators. A person does not need any education, training, or approval to become a mediator. However, most mediators are attorneys or therapists who do mediation in addition to their professional practice. You can usually feel comfortable with mediators who are lawyers or therapists, since mediation has ties to both professions. If your state does license mediators, be sure to seek out one who is licensed.

An attorney mediator can prepare an actual settlement agreement that can be submitted to the court after review by your own attorneys. Mediators with other backgrounds can only prepare memoranda of agreement, and your own attorneys must prepare the settlement document for the court.

Questions to Ask a Mediator
- How long have you done mediation?
- What are your qualifications?
  - What kind of training have you received?
  - How many divorce mediation cases have you handled?
- How long does the average case take to resolve?
- How often do you meet with a couple? How long is each session?
- Are fees charged hourly?
- What is your hourly rate?
- Is there a retainer?
- What kind of agreement do you prepare at the end of the mediation program?

Questions to Ask Yourself
- Did I feel comfortable in the office?
- Is the mediator someone I can trust and feel comfortable with?
  - Does the mediator seem to be impartial and unbiased?
- Am I comfortable with the process of mediation as the mediator explained it?
- Will I be able to be honest and open during mediation?
- Do I trust my spouse to be honest and offer full financial disclosure during mediation?
- Am I going to be able to say what I want and stand up for what I need during mediation?

The Mediation Process

Most divorces can be settled in seven to ten mediation sessions. When you agree to work with a mediator, you will sign an agreement that outlines the fee arrangement (usually a retainer with an hourly rate), the mediator's responsibilities, and your responsibilities. Because mediation is meant to be a safe place, couples with a history of domestic violence are not candidates for this process, and most mediators set rules for how the spouses may treat each other during the sessions, emphasizing respect and restraint.

The mediator usually makes it clear that he or she is only a guide and that the couple must do the actual work of finding a settlement. The mediator can provide legal information but cannot give either party personal legal advice. For this reason, both spouses must have separate attorneys to consult throughout the process. The attorneys will also review the agreement that is reached.

Both spouses must agree to make full financial disclosure to each other during mediation, just as they would in court. This means you have to provide each other with complete information about your assets and debts.

Once the mediation process has ended, the mediator will prepare a document laying out the terms of the settlement agreement. One spouse's attorney will then take the settlement to court.

Here are ways you can make mediation successful:

- Keep all appointments.
- Take time to think through all important issues.
- Avoid knee-jerk reactions when possible.
- Try not to push your spouse's buttons.
- Make decisions about custody based on what is best for your children.
- Do any homework your mediator assigns.
- Provide full financial disclosure.
- Offer alternatives and creative solutions.
- Be honest about your preferences.
- Talk to your attorney about your settlement options in court before you mediate.
- Choose a mediator you are comfortable with.
- Decide at the beginning how you and your spouse will pay for mediation (whether you will split the cost or one of you will pay for all of it).
- Stay focused on the big picture and don't get hung up on small decisions.

Keep in mind that although mediation can be therapeutic, it is not therapy. Make the best use of your mediator's time by trying to work toward solutions. If there are big issues you can't get past, see a therapist alone or with your ex to work through them.

Arbitration

Arbitration is usually thought of as an alternative to court for cases such as labor disputes. In those situations, parties can have their case decided by an arbitrator in much the same way a judge would rule on proceedings. Arbitration for matrimonial cases is still unusual, but programs in some areas are becoming popular. In these programs, cases are sent to a neutral evaluator (usually an experienced divorce attorney or retired judge) who evaluates them with both attorneys present and offers a nonbinding opinion on how a judge would decide the case. The parties and their attorneys use this information to come to a settlement.

If you're interested in arbitration, ask your attorney if this type of program is available in your area. It is often used when one or both parties just won't settle, as a last-ditch effort to avoid a trial, and can give you the peace of mind that comes with having someone experienced in this area give an unbiased opinion.

Collaborative Law

Collaborative law, discussed in Chapter 3, is a fairly new field that is becoming increasingly popular. In collaborative law, each party hires an attorney who specializes in collaborative divorce, and the attorneys work together to reach a settlement. Reaching a settlement is their only goal. This process works well for spouses who prefer a mediation-like approach but don't want to negotiate for themselves. If a settlement cannot be reached using the collaborative law process, the parties must find new lawyers who will handle the court case, because a collaborative lawyer does not handle contested cases in court.

To find a collaborative lawyer, contact your local or state bar association referral program.

Settlements

Most cases end with a settlement. Yours probably will too, although it may not come until the very last second. Settlements can be the best result for several reasons:

- Both parties feel like they have won in some way.
- Neither spouse has to say unpleasant things about the other in court.
- Settlements cost less than lengthy trials.
- A settlement fits your needs and situation, while decisions by judges are often less personal.

As you progress through your case, your attorney will probably be working constantly to reach some kind of settlement, and he or she will come to you from time to time with different proposals. Your attorney will advise you as to what is reasonable in your case, but you'll be the one who ultimately decides whether or not to accept a settlement. It's important that you not let your attorney pressure you into an arrangement you are uncomfortable with or one that does not meet your needs. You will always be balancing the settlement against what your attorney thinks a judge might decide in your case and what you really want. By its very nature a settlement is a compromise. You won't get everything you want, but you should end up with something you can live with.

It is also possible that you and your spouse will be able to talk and reach a settlement together. Doing so will save you the most money. You can tell your attorney the terms of the agreement, and as long as both attorneys approve it, it can go to court and be approved there. See Chapter 11 for more information about creating and working through settlements.

7

Gathering Household and Personal Documents

Documentation is an important part of the divorce process. Because so much of your divorce deals with financial and property matters, you need to put together and prepare to share paperwork and documentation that corresponds to your household and personal affairs. This is important because you need to provide evidence of how much money you and your spouse have, how much debt you have, what your monthly living expenses are (essential when determining child support), and what other property you own.

It can feel dehumanizing to realize that most of your divorce comes down to money and belongings, but remember that you need money and financial assets to help you live after the process is over. The legal part of divorce really is primarily a financial transaction. While it can be tempting to get fed up with the constant discussions about money and debts, you need to stay focused and try to provide as much documentation as you can in order to protect yourself. There is a direct payoff in monetary terms: the more proof you can provide, the better your chances of getting a financial settlement or decision that is in your favor. Do the work to get the payoff.

Some couples are able to see a way to divide things fairly. Others fight tooth and nail over every last knickknack and spoon. In both situations, it's really important to provide your attorney with complete and accurate records. It's not uncommon to find that although you've agreed to split things in an equal way, your spouse is holding back some assets or information you need to know. It is also important to make sure your attorney has all the information so he or she can make a recommendation. Your spouse may convince you something is a fair split when it actually isn't—your attorney needs to have all the facts and data to be able to advise you well. The only way to protect yourself (and your children if you have them) is to be thorough.

How to Gather Documentation

There are several steps involved in gathering the paperwork you need. Many items—such as bank statements, credit cards, mortgage information, car loans, insurance information, utility bills, Social Security numbers, and investment statements—are usually readily available in your household files, on your computer, or online. Other original documents, such as life insurance policies, deeds, titles, stocks, bonds, and even cash, are sometimes kept in a fireproof safe in the home or in a safe-deposit box, so be sure to check there.

You need to locate statements from the last twelve months, if possible. If your spouse has made substantial withdrawals from accounts or investments within the last several years, you will want to provide documentation of this, particularly if the money was invested in his or her business, or he or she spent it individually.

As you go through the Checklist of Documents to Gather at the end of this chapter, check off the documents you have located, then begin locating the ones you don't have. If you're missing current statements from banks, credit cards, loans, insurance companies, investments, or utility companies, look online.

Note that the checklist includes lots of things you probably hadn't thought of as marital property, such as frequent flier miles and gym memberships. These are all things of value, so find as many of them as you can (even if you don't personally have any interest in keeping them), since they will add to the pot of money and possessions to be divided. Make sure your documentation clearly shows the value, if possible. Your goal is to find as much value as humanly possible—the more you find, the bigger your share will be.

Working with Your Spouse

Since both you and your spouse have attorneys, you're going to need two copies of each document. If one of you raids the files first or goes online and changes the password, the other will have no immediate access. Sure, doing this is a way to get back at your spouse, but he or she will eventually be able to get joint account information or your spouse's attorney will obtain access to the missing documents, either through a process called discovery (when both sides in a case share requested information) or by subpoenaing the information from the company itself. Having an attorney chase down these documents will cost money. Although the bill for that work will go to your spouse, it will come out of the pot of money you're dividing, ultimately leaving less to be divided, which hurts you. Additionally, your attorney will generate billable hours responding to the request for the documents, which will come directly out of your pocket. It's more cost-effective to just allow access, as long as your lawyer agrees the documents contain information that needs to be shared. If you are trying to conceal assets or income from your spouse, discuss this with your attorney before doing anything.

When You Can't Get Certain Documents

You may not be able to find or access certain documents. For example, if your spouse owns a business, he or she will probably be advised by his or her attorney to make sure you can't access the business's financial information. You also won't be able to access information from your spouse's employer or information about any individual bank or investment accounts or credit cards your spouse holds in his or her name alone. This is information your attorney will obtain for you. If you are able to get your hands on information about these things, download them or make copies—don't take originals.

Organizing Documents

Once you have gathered the items on the checklist, you need to organize them. First make a copy of everything, whether digital or in print. Give one copy to your attorney and keep one for yourself as a backup. You will probably need to create separate hard copy or digital files for each of the subcategories listed in this chapter. Keep all the hard copy folders in the section of your accordion folder labeled "Household Documents," and keep digital files similarly labeled and organized. It is not a good idea to place originals of titles, birth certificates, or other important documents in your accordion folder. Keep the originals in a safe place at home or in your safe-deposit box, and place copies in your accordion folder. Make copies for your attorney as needed.

Next you need to sort the documents. Put household expenses together. Place bank statements together. Gather credit card bills together. Put retirement and investment income together. Try to keep them in chronological order, and if you are saving them digitally, put the month and year in the document name.

Since divorce is a lengthy process, you will constantly be obtaining new documents as bills and statements come or post each month. Stay on top of them by saving them in the right file or storing them in your accordion folder with the other relevant documents. This way you will always have current information in one place. Your attorney will not need copies of all of these documents. For example, he or she is not going to need a copy of your cable bill but will need copies of investments and bank accounts, as well as outstanding debts. You need to keep all of these documents, though, because if they are ever challenged by your spouse as part of your calculation of your monthly budget that you provide to the court, you need to be able to prove the amounts. It might seem overcautious to keep everything, but you only need to do this while your divorce is pending.

Analyzing Value

Your attorney will analyze the documents you bring him or her but also needs to have some sense of the value of the items involved. For example, while the deed to your home gives your attorney basic information about ownership, it offers no actual value for the property. A fair market rate has to be determined in order to create a property settlement. To reduce your attorney costs, you can do some of this legwork yourself.

- **Get a market value for your home.** Have a real estate agent come, and pretend you are interested in selling. He or she will bring a printout of what similar homes have sold for in your area ("comps"). This will narrow down the value of your home. You can also use http://www.zillow.com to see what homes in your area have sold for or what their estimated worth is.
- **Look up Kelley Blue Book values.** Go to the library or online at http://www.kbb .com, and find out the Blue Book values of any automobiles you and your spouse own. Locate guides for other items as well, such as boats, RVs, and motorcycles.
- **Use pricing guides.** If you and your spouse have valuable collections, use collector's guides to determine how much they are worth, or consider paying for an appraisal by an expert. If you have purchase receipts for these items (or you have had them appraised in the past, perhaps for insurance reasons), they will be very useful in proving value, so be sure to make copies for your attorney.
- **Locate your homeowner's or renter's insurance policy** (the actual policy, not just the bill). You probably have a value included on that policy for the contents of your home, and you may even have a rider to cover additional expensive items. Make sure your attorney receives a copy of this, as it can be used to prove the total net value of your marital property.
- **Locate resale values for some items.** If you have larger household items that can't easily be valued any other way (there is no Blue Book listing, and it is not something you want to pay an appraiser for), find some online pricing for comparable items sold in the same condition to show reasonable value. These might include original artwork, exercise equipment, or quirky collections.

CHECKLIST OF DOCUMENTS TO GATHER

Personal
Personal documents are used to prove identity, Social Security number, address, and dates of birth and marriage.

☐ Social Security cards for you, your spouse, and your children (Writing down the numbers is sufficient.)

☐ Marriage license

☐ Life insurance policies

☐ Birth certificates for you, your spouse, and your children

Household
Household documents are used to prove living expenses and the cost of maintaining your household.

☐ Mortgage statement

☐ Home equity loan statement

☐ Homeowner's or renter's insurance bill

☐ Lease (if you're renting)

☐ Car insurance bill

☐ Electric bills

☐ Gas bills

☐ Water bills

☐ Cable bills

☐ Internet access bills

☐ Landline phone bills

☐ Cell phone bills

☐ Any outstanding home repair or contractor bills

☐ Documentation showing the reasonable resale value for some household items

Financial
Your attorney uses a wide range of documents to prove financial net worth.

☐ Checking account statements

☐ Savings account statements

☐ Children's bank account statements

continued ▶

- [ ] Other bank account statements

- [ ] Credit union statements

- [ ] Total of cash stored in the home and elsewhere

- [ ] Investment statements

- [ ] Copies of stocks and bonds

- [ ] Retirement account statements (IRAs, Keogh plans, 401(k)s, military pensions and military retired pay, other)

- [ ] Annuities

- [ ] 529 college savings plan statements

- [ ] Trust paperwork

- [ ] Tax returns for the last five years

- [ ] Financial statements completed (such as loan applications)

Health Care

These documents will help your attorney establish your current health care insurance coverage, any contributions you've made, as well as outstanding medical bills that will need to be paid.

- [ ] Health insurance card

- [ ] Dental insurance card

- [ ] Vision insurance card

- [ ] Unpaid bills from health care providers

- [ ] Pay stubs showing amounts you contribute for insurance

Debt

These documents will help your attorney establish your total current marital debt so that it can be divided.

- [ ] Visa statements

- [ ] MasterCard statements

- [ ] Discover Card statements

- [ ] American Express statements

- [ ] Diners Club statements

- [ ] Store credit card statements

- [ ] Other credit card statements

- [ ] Personal loan statements

☐ Car loan statements

☐ Other loan statements

☐ Evidence of family loans

Employment and Income
Your attorney needs documentation to verify your and your spouse's income and benefits.

☐ Your payroll statements for the last month

☐ Your spouse's payroll statements for the last month

☐ Commission or bonus statements from the last year

☐ Reimbursed business expenses

☐ Consulting or freelance income

☐ Other benefits

☐ eBay, Amazon, and other online resale income

Self-Owned Businesses
Documentation will help your attorney value the worth of businesses you or your spouse own.

☐ Balance sheets

☐ Accounts receivable

☐ Accounts payable

☐ Bank statements

☐ Tax returns

☐ Contracts

☐ Offers to purchase the business

☐ Profit-and-loss statements

Titles and Deeds
Deeds and titles will prove the existence of large assets such as real estate and vehicles.

☐ Your car title

☐ Your spouse's car title

☐ Other vehicle titles

☐ Boat or motorcycle title

☐ Deed to the home and other real estate

☐ Tax bill for real estate

continued ▶

Other

Don't overlook your less obvious assets.

☐ Frequent flier miles

☐ Loyalty club or reward points

☐ Season tickets

☐ Time-shares

☐ Flexible spending accounts (FSAs) and health savings accounts (HSAs)

☐ Child care savings accounts

☐ Stock options

☐ Gym or club memberships

☐ Patents, copyrights, royalties, and license agreements

☐ Homeowner's or renter's insurance policies indicating the value of home contents or any riders for expensive items

8

Documenting Your Income and Living Expenses

If you have children, you will be required to provide details about your monthly living expenses to help calculate child support. Your monthly expenses are also important if you are seeking alimony or spousal support. In most states, you have to complete a financial affidavit that lists all of your income and expenses and shows a monthly living expense amount, whether or not alimony and child support are at issue.

While most people have a general sense of how much they spend per month, most don't usually have a detailed monthly budget or list of expenditures. To provide the court with accurate information, you need to create such a monthly budget for your living expenses. Many people find that this is actually an enlightening exercise; they learn a lot about their habits and are better able to control their expenses after seeing what they're really spending their money on. Creating a budget is also useful for you personally, because after the divorce, you'll be responsible for all of these expenses yourself. Getting a sense of what they are now can help you plan for the postdivorce period.

How to Document Expenses and Income

While it is usually acceptable to estimate some portions of your monthly expenses for the court's purposes, doing a true expense log is a helpful exercise for you and your attorney, because it gives you a realistic number to work with. At the end of this chapter, you will find an Income Log and an Expense Log. Use them to record all of your income and expenses for one calendar month. If you prefer, you can set up a computer spreadsheet to record your expenses.

When completing the Income Log, record only the income that you bring into your household. This includes all of your reportable income for the month. It does not include

IRREGULAR EXPENSES

Make notes of contracts for things like cable, Internet, and cell phones where you may have short-term special pricing. Include what the future increased price will be on your budget.

Go through your checkbook, online banking, and credit card statements for the past year to look for expenses that happen only a few times a year, such as upgrading your cell phone, renewing your driver's license, or having your septic tank pumped.

garage sale or eBay income unless those kinds of sales are your business. You can choose to record pretax or after-tax income, but if you record pretax income, you will need to list taxes and other payroll deductions on the Expense Log.

You can store all of your pay statements or income receipts in the "Income Documents" pocket of your accordion file and then record them all at the end of the month, or you can keep them all in a separate digital folder. If you're using paper documents, make sure you transfer these to the "Household Documents" pocket once you have recorded all of the income for the month. If you're using digital statements, copy them into the "Household Documents" folder.

Using the Expense Log, record every expense you pay over the one-month period. This includes checks you write, bills you pay, online payments, payment made via debit, automatic payments, and items you purchase in cash. Credit card expenses should be recorded when you pay the bill, not when the charges are incurred. You might want to keep a running tally in your wallet, purse, or phone to track cash expenditures—you'll be surprised at how they add up. Total all expenses at the end of the month.

Note that this log may not be an accurate reflection of what your financial situation will be after the divorce. For example, if your spouse is currently making the mortgage payments on your home and you're living in it, you won't have anything recorded on your log for rent or mortgage. Or you may be paying the car insurance bill, which includes both your car and your spouse's. This is fine, as long as you make a note of all the things that are not reflected in your log, as well as the things that are listed but will change after the divorce, so that your attorney can understand. You will want to include these expenses on your form for the court, so the judge can see what it will actually cost you to live in your home after the divorce.

If you and your spouse are still living together, you may need to estimate what your costs will be when you do finally physically separate. If you are planning to move out, estimate what your expenses will be in an apartment or rental house. If you are planning to buy a new home, you'll need to estimate those costs as well. If your spouse is going to move out, determine if this will lower the monthly household costs (for example, your food costs will likely decrease, and the cell phone bill should be separated into two accounts).

Now comes the ugly part. Compare your total monthly income to your total monthly expenses. Don't panic if your expenses are higher than your income. This often happens, and it means that you overestimated something or that you are relying on your spouse's income. In practical terms, it's good for your case, because it demonstrates that you don't have a lot of money to spend on alimony or child support or, conversely, that you need financial support.

Creating a Budget

Once you know how much you're really spending, use the numbers to create a budget. A budget is an estimated list of monthly expenses. While the Expense Log gives you a snapshot of what you spend each month, a budget gives an average monthly total and includes the average amount of expenses that are paid on a yearly or quarterly basis. This budget is what you will use to complete divorce-related paperwork.

To create a budget, go through each item on the Monthly Budget worksheet and list an average monthly amount. If you have not separated, use your current joint living expenses. If you have separated, use your single expenses. Remember that specific costs, such as gas or electricity, go up at certain times of the year. Use average monthly costs for things that you pay less frequently than monthly, such as vacation expenses, holiday gifts, car registration fees, license renewal costs, club memberships, and so on. Come up with a yearly total for these and divide by twelve to find an average monthly figure. You can also use a computer spreadsheet to create your budget, but be sure to use the categories from the budget form.

Some items in the budget may not apply to you. For example, if your children will not be living with you full-time, you may not be responsible for some of their expenses (at least until you start paying child support). Don't forget that this budget is supposed to be for you as a single person (or as a single head of household if you have kids), so don't include things such as your spouse's magazine subscriptions or his or her car expenses. If you are unsure who will be handling certain joint expenses such as credit cards, home equity loans, and other payments, leave them off, but be sure to mention them to your attorney. Use the Unresolved Joint Expenses form to document these items. Including them in your budget implies that you intend to take full responsibility for them after the divorce, and that's not an impression you want to give. Also include all expenses for everyone who will continue to live in your household. So, for example, where the form asks for tuition, you would include tuition for yourself as well as for your children.

Once you have completed the Monthly Budget worksheet, total it to obtain an average monthly living expense. Now take a few minutes to think about it. Are there places you can cut expenses? Think about what you can do to improve your financial picture once your divorce is over and you're on your own. Remember that if alimony or child support is an issue in your case, it is generally a good strategy to make it appear as if your monthly expenses are large. This doesn't mean you should artificially inflate them, but it is a good idea to err on the side of high estimates as opposed to low ones.

INCOME LOG

Print copies of this log for further use. List all actual income you bring into the household this month.

Income Log for the Month of _____

Date	Type/Description	Amount
	TOTAL	

Print copies of this log for further use. It should include all the expenses you actually pay for your household, including those for your children.

Expense Log for the Month of _____

Date	Type/Description	Amount
TOTAL		

MONTHLY BUDGET ▶

Household

Rent/mortgage   _____

Home equity loan payments   _____

Real estate taxes (if not included in mortgage)   _____

Homeowner's (if not included in mortgage) or renter's insurance   _____

Homeowner's association fees   _____

Gas   _____

Water   _____

Electricity   _____

Telephone (local and long-distance calls)   _____

Cell phone   _____

Internet access, e-mail, and data plans   _____

Cable   _____

Computer and technology supplies, costs, and repairs   _____

Home repairs   _____

Appliances and appliance maintenance   _____

Food (include takeout but not dining out)   _____

Alcohol (include home supplies but not bars or restaurants)   _____

Household supplies (cleaning supplies, home office supplies,
    paper goods, and items like wood for fireplaces and so on)   _____

Children's allowances   _____

Pet food and supplies   _____

Vet, boarding, and grooming expenses   _____

Household help (such as cleaning, lawn service, dog walking,
    and laundry)   _____

Charitable donations   _____

Furniture purchases or maintenance   _____

Lawn and yard expenses   _____

Other _____   _____

Personal

Clothing and shoes   _____

Personal care supplies (toiletries and so on)   _____

Coin laundry and dry cleaning   _____

Haircuts and styling   _____

Gym membership   _____

Personal care (nails, salon, facials, shoe shine/repair,
    massage, acupuncture)   _____

Other club memberships   _____

Life insurance premiums   _____

Health insurance premiums   _____

Health insurance copayments   _____

Prescription costs   _____

Over-the-counter medications   _____

Vision care costs (eye examinations as well as contacts
    and eyeglasses)   _____

Dental costs   _____

Medical supplies or equipment   _____

Hobbies and activities   _____

Tobacco expenses   _____

Other _____   _____

Financial

Monthly contributions to retirement accounts   _____

Taxes   _____

Bank charges   _____

Finance charges on credit cards   _____

Payments and finance charges on personal loans   _____

Monthly contributions to flexible spending accounts (FSAs)
    and health savings accounts (HSAs)   _____

Other monthly deductions from pay not included elsewhere   _____

Transportation

Car loan or lease payment   _____

Auto insurance   _____

Repairs and maintenance (monthly average)   _____

Average for license, inspection, and registration   _____

Bus, taxi, train, and/or plane costs   _____

Gas   _____

Car washes   _____

Parking, parking permits, tolls, and E-Z passes   _____

Expenses for other vehicles (include boat, motorcycle, RV,
    and other cars)   _____

Other _____   _____

Entertainment

Dining/drinking out   _____

Movies, theater, shows, and attractions   _____

Books, newspapers, magazines, and e-books   _____

Music downloads, music subscriptions, and radio subscriptions   _____

Gaming   _____

Movie rentals and subscriptions   _____

Vacation   _____

Babysitters   _____

Other _____   _____

Gifts

Holiday gifts (include average for all holidays you buy gifts for)   _____

Birthday, anniversary, wedding, baby, hostess, and retirement gifts   _____

continued ▶

Cards, wrapping paper, gift bags, decorations, and supplies _____

Office gift collections _____

Other _____ _____

School

Tuition _____

School books and supplies _____

Student loan payments _____

Activities, lessons, and sports fees _____

Uniforms and equipment _____

Field trips and other special school expenses _____

Day care _____

After-school day care _____

Other

_____

_____ _____

_____ _____

_____ _____

_____ _____

_____ _____

_____ _____

_____ _____

_____ _____

_____ _____

_____ _____

_____ _____

_____ _____

_____ _____

_____ _____

_____ _____

_____ _____

UNRESOLVED JOINT EXPENSES

Description	Amount

9

Large Assets

Dividing large or important assets fairly can be difficult, because they may not be things you can easily cut in half or because the value of one large asset may be greater than the total of all your other assets. Contested divorces often include division of pensions, investments, vehicles, homes, and second homes, as well as the value of businesses, professional licenses, and degrees. Future potential earnings aren't divided as assets, but they are part of the consideration for alimony.

Because your large assets are worth so much, you want to gather as much information about them as you can to maximize your settlement or award. Accurate valuations are also important so these items can be divided fairly.

Separate Versus Marital Property

The first step in property division is determining which large assets are separate property and which are marital property. Things that were acquired during the marriage—even if they are owned in one name only—are usually *marital property* and must be considered in your property division. *Separate property*, sometimes called premarital property, cannot be divided in a divorce. It includes things owned before the marriage, received through gift or inheritance during the marriage, or awarded as a personal injury settlement during the marriage.

There's one point you need to know about separate property: a portion of the value of an item that is separate property can be considered marital property if the nonowner spouse contributed to its upkeep or increased its value during marriage. Assume, for example, that you owned a home before you were married and rented it out to tenants while you were married. If your spouse painted, mowed the lawn, or fixed the plumbing while you were married, he or she contributed to the upkeep of that property and would be entitled to receive a portion of the increase in its value that occurred because of his or her input. Additionally, if you used marital assets (income earned by either of you during your marriage) or your spouse used separate assets to pay the mortgage, part of the value of that home becomes marital property. Similarly, if your spouse owned a business prior to your marriage and you helped out at the business while you were married (and did not receive a salary for the work you did), you would be entitled to a portion of the increase in value that occurred during that time.

If you are the nonowner spouse, use the Contribution to Separate Asset worksheet at the end of this chapter to document your involvement with the asset. Write down all the ways you've assisted with or contributed to an asset that your spouse owns separately. Note how much marital money was put into the asset during your marriage. Also note any contributions by your spouse to your separate assets, so your attorney can be aware of them. Use the Large Asset as Separate Property Log at the end of the chapter to document items you own separately.

Understanding Nonconcrete Assets

Everything acquired during a marriage (not acquired through separate gift, inheritance, or personal injury award) is considered marital property and is subject to division. This includes intangibles such as degrees, professional licenses, businesses, retirement accounts, websites, digital assets, and even frequent flier miles.

A degree or professional license that was earned while you were married, such as a medical degree or a license to style hair, is considered marital property, even though it is not technically "divided" in a divorce settlement. The court can't give you your spouse's MBA, but its value can be included in the total pot of assets, and you will probably be entitled to some cash value if you provided support while he or she was earning that license or degree. Even if your spouse is not currently using the degree (he or she is still in school, for example, or is staying home with the children), it is still an item of property with a value. After all, should he or she put the degree to use sometime in the future, it will enhance his or her earning power.

How Large Assets Are Divided

82

How the court divides your assets and debts depends on your state laws. In some states, all assets and debts are split exactly in half. In others, the court divides them based on what is fair in that particular situation.

When a property settlement or division is made in your case, you won't each get half of every asset. It would be difficult—and often impossible—to give each spouse one-half of a car, a house, a business, or a degree. Instead, all of the assets will be valued and totaled, and you will each receive half of the total value or whatever amount a court decides is equitable (fair). One of you might get the house, for example, while the other might get the investments. Large assets are often balanced with debt. The spouse who gets the house might also be solely responsible for the mortgage. It is also possible to continue to jointly own some assets, as is discussed later in this chapter. It important that you make it clear to your lawyer what your preferences are—what you would like to be awarded in the divorce so that the settlement can be structured in this way.

Finding Large Assets

To ensure that your property division will be fair (and that you will get as much as possible), you need to create a complete list of large marital assets. Use the List of Large Joint Assets at the end of this chapter for that purpose.

Get together all account statements. If you need information on your or your spouse's retirement accounts or pension plan, call the plan administrator and request a current statement or check online. If you are unable to access your spouse's information, just make a note that the account exists and include all the information you know. Your attorney will be able to obtain the details.

Think carefully about intangible assets such as licenses, degrees, and businesses—as mentioned earlier, they may have value. If you list professional licenses or degrees, indicate what they are and the dates they were awarded. For a degree, indicate the years it took to earn it and how much the tuition was. If training was involved in obtaining a professional license, indicate that and any costs involved.

Also include items that you may not consider important. For example, if your spouse has a motorcycle or a collection of Depression glass, you should list these items even if you have no interest in them, because they increase the total pot of assets.

Finding Hidden Assets

You might think it is difficult to hide high-value assets, but many spouses have done so. It is particularly easy to do if one spouse has a business. Joint assets or funds can

VALUING ONLINE ASSETS

If you or your spouse writes a blog, has a website, or sells things online, those digital items are marital property. They have a value, and that value should be counted as part of your divorce. If you are the one with the online asset, you want to minimize its value. Portray it as a hobby. If your ex is the one with the asset, you want to show that it has some actual value. A website that relates to a brick-and-mortar business is one more asset of that company. A blog that earns any money directly (from ads or sponsorships) or indirectly (by driving business to your ex in any way) also has a value.

Be sure to note if you have contributed to developing or improving the asset your spouse will want to claim: did you write blog posts, design a website, promote it via social media, schedule social media updates for it? This kind of work will indicate that you are entitled to a portion of the value of the asset.

Social media accounts are also marital assets and may have a value if they drive business or income, so be sure to consider this. No matter what the value of these accounts is, it's a good idea to ask your attorney to have your decree or settlement agreement specify that you will own your own blogs, website, social media accounts, and digital assets as part of the divorce. List all of these online assets on the Online Assets form.

be funneled into the business to hide them from the other spouse. You should also be suspicious if your spouse has recently taken a trip to a foreign country, where it may be possible to conceal cash in secret bank accounts. In most cases, though, you'll probably sense if your spouse is trying to hide something. If you do believe he or she is hiding a large amount of money, talk to your attorney about the possibility of hiring a private investigator to track it down.

Make hard copies or save digital copies of all account statements you can find, especially those that are in your spouse's name alone. Make note of large cash withdrawals from joint or sole accounts. Cash is hard to trace, but if you can prove that your spouse has withdrawn it, you have a convincing piece of evidence.

Documenting and Dividing Large Assets

There are different types of large assets, and you will need to obtain different information for each of them.

Accounts

Assets such as investments, bank accounts, and CDs can be easy to value. All you need is an account statement. These accounts can simply be closed and the cash distributed between you and your spouse. If you have joint CDs, it might make sense to keep them until maturity to avoid penalties, then divide them.

Retirement Accounts

You have two choices when dividing pensions and retirement accounts (including IRAs and 401(k)s, as well as military retired pay). You can determine a current cash value (what the account is worth today), for which you will need an accountant, and give the nontitled spouse a portion of that value. Or you can agree that the nontitled spouse will receive a certain percentage of the payments when they are made at retirement.

If you are the owner, you may prefer to settle up now so you won't have to worry about it later, but it sometimes makes more sense to choose the long-term approach. If you or your spouse should die before retirement, no payments will be made.

If you are the nonowner spouse, a bird in the hand may be better than two in the bush in this case. If you take a cash settlement now, you can invest it or do what you like with it. If you choose to wait, you or your spouse might die before retirement, leaving you with nothing. As always, this is a choice you should discuss with your attorney before making any decisions, and it is usually a good idea to consult a specialist who can calculate the values of these accounts and make a recommendation.

Note that Social Security accounts are considered marital assets if you have been married more than ten years. These benefits are not actually paid until retirement age, but they will be divided as part of your divorce settlement or order.

Businesses

You need a specialized accountant to value a business, and it can be an expensive and time-consuming effort, so consider how large or small the business is before you decide to go that route. It is usually a bad idea for two former spouses to continue to co-own a company after they divorce. (How would you solve business disagreements?) Talk to your attorney about this. A cash settlement or buyout may make more sense, but it depends on your particular situation.

If one of you co-owns a business with someone else, it becomes even more complicated. Technically you could divide the ownership of that fraction of the business between you, but again, it would be very difficult. Instead, you will want a careful valuation of the business and a settlement of some kind.

Real Estate

Real estate can generally be appraised by local real estate agents or real estate appraisers. You can also go to your county clerk's office and look up homes comparable to yours that have sold recently to find out what the sale price was (you will need to know the addresses to obtain this information). Another resource for finding comparable home values is http://www.zillow.com. Do not rely on your property tax assessment. While it can be a good starting point, it is often wildly different from the price you can get for a home on the market. Remember that when you value a home, you have to find out what it would sell for and then subtract the mortgage owed to determine how much value it has.

The possible ownership outcomes for real estate are as follows:

- You will own the home alone.
- Your spouse will own the home alone.
- You will sell the home and share the proceeds (if there are any).
- You and your spouse will continue to own the home jointly. This can happen in the following cases:
  - One of you will remain in the home with the children, and you agree to sell the home once they leave for college.
  - You will own the home jointly, rent it, and continue to share expenses and any profit from it.
  - You will jointly own the home until its value increases enough to sell it.

Keep in mind that continuing to own the marital home jointly will make it hard for you to buy another home for yourself if there is a mortgage on the home you own with your spouse. You also will need to agree about home repairs and share the cost of taxes.

Licenses and Degrees

You need a specialized accountant to value licenses and degrees. Sometimes these items are valued as part of a business or practice (such as a medical practice), and sometimes they are valued by themselves. Since this is a complicated area of law that varies from state to state and uses different formulas and rules, it is important to talk to your attorney.

Once you have obtained information about the value of your large assets, store the documents in the "Large Assets" pocket of your accordion file or in a folder on your computer.

CONTRIBUTION TO SEPARATE ASSET

Use this worksheet to describe your contributions to your spouse's separately owned assets during the marriage. Create a document for each asset. You should also note any contributions your spouse has made to your separate assets.

Asset _____

Contributions (approximate dates and descriptions)

_____
_____
_____
_____
_____
_____
_____
_____
_____
_____
_____
_____
_____
_____
_____
_____
_____
_____
_____
_____
_____
_____
_____
_____
_____
_____

LARGE ASSET AS SEPARATE PROPERTY LOG

List large assets that are your separate property.

Description	Value	When and How Acquired

ONLINE ASSETS

Use this form to list all blogs, websites, online stores, social media accounts, and other online presences and accounts used or owned by your or your spouse.

Type of Asset	Name/Identity/URL	How It Increases Income or Value

LIST OF LARGE JOINT ASSETS

Description	Account Number (if any)	Location	Approximate Value

10

Documenting Debts

The good news is that even though you have to divide assets in a divorce, you also get to divide your debts. Debts can be divided equally or based on considerations of fairness (this varies by state law). For example, the spouse with the higher income may be held responsible for more of the debt, or the spouse keeping the car may take on the car loan.

Separate and Marital Debts

Debts, like assets, can be separate or marital. Debts you incurred prior to your marriage will be your separate responsibility, and the same goes for your spouse, even if you worked together to pay down the premarital debts. Remember that even if a debt is listed in only one name, it is still considered a joint or marital debt if it was taken out during the marriage.

Use the List of Spouse's Separate Debts worksheet at the end of this chapter to create a list of your spouse's separate (acquired before marriage) debts so that you do not become responsible for paying them.

Organizing Your Debts

There are two kinds of debt to consider: recurring and long-term. *Recurring debts*—rent and utility bills, for example—are those that happen on a regular basis, are paid, and then occur again. Hopefully, you and your spouse are in a position to pay these bills as they arise. Recurring debts don't need to be divided, because as soon as you separate, or as soon as your divorce concludes, you will each have your own set of recurring debts and will pay them on your own. However, if you have arrears, balances, and penalties, these need to be included in your list of joint debts.

Long-term debts are the ones to be concerned about when you're facing divorce. You need to create a complete list of these debts with current balances due. Use the List of Joint Debts at the end of this chapter to organize this information. Place copies of all loan statements and other debt-related documents in the appropriate pocket of your accordion file or save copies in a folder on your computer. Even if you have included these items elsewhere, it is a good idea to keep copies of them here so you have all your debt information in one place.

When listing debts, be sure to include the following:

- Car loans and leases
- Mortgages
- Home equity loans
- Personal loans (unsecured loans)
- Student loans
- Lines of credit (such as overdrafts)
- Loans against life insurance
- Loans against retirement or pension accounts
- Loans from relatives or friends
- Credit card balances (those not paid off each month)
- Unpaid balances on utilities
- Unpaid health care bills for you, your spouse, your children, or your pets
- Judgments or liens
- Unpaid insurance bills
- Installment payments
- Late rent

Do not include business loans. These will be deducted against the value of the business.

If you are unsure of what you owe on a specific loan, call the creditor. If you think you have other debts outstanding but can't put your finger on what they are, look through your checkbook or online bank account to see to whom you make payments on a regular basis. If you still can't find the information, order your credit report. See Chapter 2 to find out how to order a credit report.

Creditor	Account Number	Current Balance

LIST OF JOINT DEBTS

Make copies of this log for further use.

Creditor	Account Number	Current Balance

11

Reaching Settlements and Dividing Property

You will find you and your spouse can divide many things on your own. Some of these agreements will be informal, small decisions, such as who will take the dishes, while others will be large decisions, such as how you will arrange custody or divide debt, that need to be incorporated into your divorce decree. This chapter will help you work out small household issues as well as larger settlements.

Negotiating Settlements

As you work through your case, use the Settlement List at the end of this chapter to organize your big household belongings into three categories—must have, unsure, and don't want. Do this for possessions as well as custody, visitation, child support, and alimony. Make sure you create a payment range for child support and alimony with the lowest and highest amounts you want to receive or pay out. Be sure you keep all of this information to yourself and don't share it with your spouse!

During negotiations, your attorney will probably advise you to pretend that you want some of the things on your don't-want and unsure lists. This strategy will allow you to bargain for things you truly must have. Never reveal your range for alimony or child support to your spouse. If you are negotiating on your own, pick a number that is less than you're willing to pay or more than you need to receive. This will give you room to negotiate.

As you move through the divorce process, you'll probably change your mind a few times about where certain items belong on your list, so be prepared to rewrite it as you go. Use the unsure column for items that you'd be willing to trade for other things you would rather have. This will help identify items to offer in a settlement.

You will need to consider all elements of your divorce in the settlement process—custody, child support, alimony, property division, and debt resolution. Settlements are complicated processes that involve careful calculations of retirement benefits, appraisal value, and income potential, as well as custody and visitation issues. You aren't always trading apples for apples, meaning that you might, for example, agree to accept a larger property settlement in exchange for less alimony. Listen to your attorney's advice about settlements, because important tax implications are involved.

Your proposal has to be reasonable or it is unlikely that your spouse, let alone a judge, will agree to it. Unless your lawyer recommends it, don't waste everyone's time proposing a settlement that gives you everything and your spouse nothing. Use these guidelines to evaluate settlement offers:

- Do I feel comfortable with the terms of the settlement?
- Am I getting everything that is really important to me?
- Does the settlement allow me to manage financially after the divorce?
- Does the settlement give me most of my must-haves?
- Have all assets and debts been taken into account and divided in the plan?
- Have I had enough time to really consider the settlement and think through its implications?
- Are the compromises things I can live with?
- Does the settlement make me feel cheated or angry?
- Do I feel pressured into settling by my attorney or spouse?

Any agreement you make with your spouse on your own is an informal settlement, meaning that it is unenforceable if one of you goes back on your word. For this reason, it is important to consult your attorney about large settlement issues and have everything formalized. Your attorney can present a settlement to the court, and the judge will incorporate it into the final divorce order. Your attorney can also draw up settlement papers that you and your spouse can sign to make an agreement official.

Dividing Household Items

Furniture, dishes, electronics, photo albums, inexpensive jewelry, and special collections carry a lot of meaning and are important items for daily living. Dividing these items can be difficult, because many of them were acquired jointly during the marriage and often have so much sentimental value. In addition, it can be quite a task to sort through everything you've accumulated while you've been married.

Separate Property

Before tackling the long list of household items that you will divide, you need to make a list of small items that are separate property. As explained in previous chapters, separate property includes items that each of you owned before your marriage, as well as items either of you received as gifts (even from each other) or inheritances during the marriage. To divide small household items of separate property, list these on the Separate Property Small Items form at the end of this chapter. These things are yours, and your spouse has no claim to them. Note that an engagement ring is usually considered separate property because it was a gift, but wedding rings are sometimes considered marital property, depending on state law.

Marital Property

Items acquired during the marriage are referred to as marital property (or community property in some states). These items belong to both of you, and during the divorce, you or the court will have to determine who gets them. In some states, property is divided in half; in others, it is divided in a way the court thinks is fair.

For many people, division of marital property becomes symbolic of the entire divorce. They want to "win" and come out with the most stuff. They take things to punish their spouse, or they rely on belongings to represent their self-worth. Try to think rationally about your possessions. Letting your spouse take the DVD player doesn't mean he or she has "won." Possessions don't symbolize anything if you don't let them. Don't view the property settlement as a way to hurt your spouse; it's not worth $200 an hour to have your attorney negotiate the division of minor things. Focus on the items you will get the most use out of or that you need the most.

The best plan is to figure out the division of most household items with your spouse, if possible. Many items will be easy to divide. You may have no interest in the big-screen TV, the sewing kit, the ceramic figurines, the ironing board, or the power tools.

Follow these suggestions when dividing things:

- Try not to break up sets (such as a matching couch and loveseat or a set of china). Sets have more value when they are together. That being said, if you have two matching frying pans, it makes sense for each of you to take one.
- Take items you want or will use. Don't take things out of spite or revenge.
- Try to keep most of the children's belongings or items they use the most in the household in which they will spend the most time.
- Make sure the household the children will live in is comfortable and safe and is outfitted so they can be well cared for.
- Recognize that you each will have to purchase replacements for some household items. No one is going to walk away from this with everything.
- Focus first on dividing items according to obvious needs; worry later about making things fair on the bottom line.
- Focus first on use, not on value. Bottom-line value can be adjusted later.
- Your lifestyle is going to be different after your divorce, so focus on what you will need in your new life and leave behind things that are part of your old life. This is a great opportunity for reinvention.
- Keep track of who has taken what. Two months from now, you're not going to remember, and it will affect the bottom-line value.

PETS

For many people, pets are like children. However, the court considers them property. It's usually best if you and your spouse can come to an agreement about who should own the pets after the divorce. If there are children, it usually makes sense for the pets to live where the children live. It's possible to own pets jointly after a divorce, and some people even create "visitation" schedules for pets so that both spouses can continue to spend time with them. If you can't agree about your pets, your best solution is to see a mediator who can help you come to an agreement. A court is unlikely to provide a lot of time or consideration for pet custody.

Note that if your pet is very valuable (a show dog, for example), it will need to be included as an asset of the marriage with a value attached.

Use this as an opportunity to purge your belongings. As you sort through things, try to be sensitive to what your spouse wants to keep. Though you might think a football jersey or a ceramic bear is worthless, he or she might want it. Throw out only those items you know no one wants. Donate items that are in good condition to a charity (such as Goodwill or the Salvation Army) and get a receipt to use as a tax deduction. You might also consider holding a garage sale or selling things on eBay and splitting the proceeds.

The division of household items usually begins before the divorce does, and it occurs not in an afternoon, but over a period of months. One spouse moves out and takes some things. Over the following weeks, he or she comes back for more items, a few at a time. You should be thinking about bottom-line value equality, so document this ongoing property division.

Problems can also arise when one spouse takes items without telling the other. If this happens to you, it is a long, hard road to get these items back. List everything you think is missing on the form titled Items Taken Without Agreement, and give the list to your attorney. Your attorney will work to get some items returned by agreement or will include these items in the things you are asking the court to award to you. Otherwise, these items will be included in the total net worth of all assets, so you will at least receive half of their value. Once you have divided the undisputed items, fill out the Agreed-Upon Items to Divide list to specify who gets what. It's a good idea for both of you to initial or sign the list to indicate your agreement. This will be useful in resolving future disputes and will help you create a fair overall division of items.

Appraising Items

Although you probably have some idea of what each item cost when you bought it or what it would sell for new today, in a divorce you need to come up with a value that reflects an item's actual condition and age. The couch you paid $3,000 for when it was new may be worth only $400 if you were to resell it now. If you don't know what something is worth, look in the classifieds or on eBay or Craigslist. EBay allows you to search for what things sold for (do an advanced search and choose completed items).

Although as a practical matter you'll probably be splitting up most of your marital property, things that can be classified as sets or collections have a greater value together than they would if valued singly and added together. Following are some items that can be valued as groups:

- Books
- CDs and DVDs
- China and dishes
- Cookware
- Glassware
- Holiday decorations
- Household art/paintings
- Houseplants
- Items in a collection (such as sports memorabilia or figurines)
- Lawn and garden tools
- Linens and towels
- Sets of furniture
- Silverware
- Software
- Tools

When it comes to negotiating, you always want to value the items your spouse is taking at a higher value than the items you're taking, if possible.

Digital Property

Another category of items you need to think about and divide is digital property. This could include the following:

- Apps
- Digital music, movies, and TV shows
- Digital photos
- Digital videos
- E-books

Remember, any of these items that were acquired during the marriage are considered marital property. Generally these items are easy to divide. Personal photos and videos can be copied, so no real division is necessary, although you might want to specify that you want copies of certain things. If photos or videos were purchased (such as from a stock photo site) and have limited-use issues, then they have a monetary value. E-books, music, paid apps, TV shows, and movies are harder to divide, since they often cannot be moved easily from one person's device or account to another. If there is something you feel strongly about, be sure to mention it to your attorney.

Disputed Items

Now that you've split up the uncontested items, it's time to get down to the nitty-gritty of negotiating the rest. Begin by filling out the Disputed Small Household Items to Divide list. Some couples are able to make this list together, while others find they need to do it alone to avoid arguments. Do whatever works for you. In either case, you'll probably need to negotiate the value of the items.

When you have compiled your list, make a copy of it, keeping one unmarked version for your ex. Then sit down by yourself and put a check in front of each item you definitely want. Put a question mark in front of items you would like but are willing to give up in exchange for other items.

Once you know what you want, go through the list with your spouse, using the unmarked copy, and indicate items you would like. Include the items you checked on your copy as well as some that were question marks. Act as if you really want the questionable items initially, then give them up as a compromise. If you use this tactic, though, keep in mind that your spouse knows you well and may be able to tell when you're bluffing. Your spouse will also need to go through the list and point out what he or she wants. Put the initials of the person you both agree will take each item next to it on the list.

Try to be reasonable during negotiations. Remember, these are only material possessions. It may be helpful to set some ground rules before you begin:

- Do not raise your voices or insult each other.
- Treat this as a business meeting.
- Meet without the children present.
- Meet in a neutral or private place.
- Try not to discuss other issues involved with the divorce at this time.
- Agree to stop and have another meeting if you get stuck or things get too tense.

When dividing disputed items, consider pairing up items of similar value. Suggestions like "You take the freezer, and I'll take the fridge," or "You take one dresser, and I'll take the other" can really jump-start the process. You may get down to just a few items. It can help to look at the value of the items that are left and see if there is a way to divide them so you each get an equal value. If you are unable to agree on certain items, talk to your attorney or mediator about how to divide them.

100
Total the value of the items you've each taken on the Disputed Small Household Items to Divide list, then add the total value from the list of undisputed items that you've already divided. Compare your totals. They don't have to be equal. In most states, marital property is divided in a way that is fair but not necessarily equal (sometimes called *equitable distribution*). The important thing is that you both feel the property division is fair. If you want to have a completely equal division, you will need to factor in large items, investments, real estate, and cash.

SETTLEMENT LIST

Must Have	Unsure	Don't Want

SEPARATE PROPERTY SMALL ITEMS

List items you owned prior to the marriage.

ITEMS TAKEN WITHOUT AGREEMENT

Description	Value	Date Taken

AGREED-UPON ITEMS TO DIVIDE

Item	Approximate Value	Owner

Total value of your items _____

Total value of your spouse's items _____

DISPUTED SMALL HOUSEHOLD ITEMS TO DIVIDE

Item	Approximate Value	Owner

Total value of your items _____

Total value of your spouse's items _____

12

Child Support

Child support is calculated on the basis of parental income, which is determined in most states by completing a detailed form. Once income is determined, a percentage is applied to child support based on the number of children involved. Child support has to do with children from this marriage only. Children from another marriage or relationship do not play a part in the calculation unless they have been adopted by the other spouse. Talk with your attorney about the laws in your state, and ask how child support will be calculated.

Purpose of Child Support

Child support is not meant to be a punishment for the parent paying it or a free ride for the parent receiving it. It is intended to ensure that children can maintain the same lifestyle after a divorce that they had before. Although child support is based on the parents' incomes, it is meant to benefit the kids. Even so, the parent who receives it is not required to document that the money was spent to support the children.

Temporary Child Support

A temporary order of child support is often made while the divorce case is ongoing so that the parent who is living with the children most of the time will have ongoing support. The amount is temporary until a final order of child support is handed down at the end of the case.

Calculating Child Support

If you are the parent who will be paying child support, it's important to understand that the amount is going to be calculated primarily based on your income. Child support can be paid weekly, biweekly, or monthly. As you work with your attorney, your general strategy will be to minimize your income whenever possible. The more income you show, the more you will end up paying. You must report your income honestly to the court, but your attorney can help you find ways to minimize the amount you report. You need to talk with your attorney if your spouse has knowledge of any income you don't report to the IRS. It's also important to share any long-term medical problems you have that might impact your ability to work.

Another part of your general strategy is to help the court see all of your spouse's income. Your attorney might want to imply that your spouse has a higher income or a greater earning potential than he or she is disclosing. This may seem a little under-handed, but keep in mind that the whole point is to make it appear as if your spouse does not need the amount of child support that is being requested. Tell your attorney if you're uncomfortable with this tactic.

If you are the parent who will be receiving child support, you want to minimize your income and appear to be at a lower standard of living than your spouse. If you have any long-term medical problems that could impact your ability to work, you should discuss this with your attorney. Your strategy will be to gather as much information as you can about your spouse's earnings. If you have information about unreported income, share this with your attorney. Although some people feel satisfaction in alerting the IRS to a spouse's unreported income, both spouses who sign the tax return are generally liable for these omissions. Because this can backfire, it's best to hold off on vengeful tactics like this until you can discuss the implications with your attorney.

Other Child Support Amounts

A court can raise a child support award above the base amount set by state law in response to factors such as the incomes of the parents, the lifestyle to which the child is accustomed, and the child's special needs. In many states, medical care, school tuition, uniforms, lessons, sports equipment, extracurricular expenses, and more are added to the base child support amount. The more expenses you can document, the more child support you will receive. Use the Children's Expenses form at the end of this chapter to record that information. Place corresponding receipts in the accordion folder pocket or digital folder labeled "Children's Expenses." If you are the parent who will be paying child support, you want to minimize the expenses presented by your spouse as much as possible, keeping in mind that the goal is to make sure your kids are supported adequately. While you do pay child support to your ex, the money is used to pay for your children's home and living expenses, so don't lose sight of this.

Most states require one parent to be responsible for providing health insurance for the child—normally whoever has family coverage available through an employer. The non-custodial parent—the one who pays child support—may have to pay health care expenses not covered by insurance as well (note that this includes copays and coinsurance, as well as things that are simply not covered). The court may also order the noncustodial parent to take out a life insurance policy on him- or herself with the child as beneficiary. This is intended to provide ongoing financial support for the child if that parent dies and child support ends.

If you are the parent receiving child support and the other parent is required to pay uninsured health care expenses, you need to keep careful records of your children's uninsured medical expenses. The best method is to inform the provider that the other parent bears the financial responsibility and that he or she is to be billed directly for any uninsured expenses. Be aware that if you have things set up this way and your ex fails to pay the bills, the health care provider might refuse to see your child.

Unexpected health care problems do arise, and many providers require copayments to be made at the time of service. Pharmacies also require payment at pickup. In these instances, you may have to pay the expense out of pocket and seek repayment from the other parent. Use the Children's Uninsured Health Expenses form to record expenses and repayment. Give your spouse copies of the form and the receipts each month. Store originals in the accordion folder pocket labeled "Children's Uninsured Health Care Receipts" or keep electronic copies in a file on your computer until they have been paid.

How Child Support Is Paid

Child support can be paid directly by one parent to the other, or it can be paid to a state child support collection agency, which then pays the custodial parent. Payments to the state are usually made via automatic paycheck deduction.

Some judges will automatically order payments to be made through the state, while others may let the parties decide. Generally, if you are the person receiving child support, it is to your benefit to have it go through the state. The state will keep track of the payments and will contact the other parent if payments are missing. You won't have to discuss child support with your spouse because he or she will deal with the state, thus removing a lot of the conflict from your contact with each other. These agencies usually review and adjust the payment amounts on a regular basis to keep pace with inflation.

If you are the person paying child support, you may not want to have payments taken out of your paycheck. Some people are uncomfortable with their employer knowing their personal business. Also, if you make payments directly to the other parent, he or she will probably be forgiving if you are a day or two late in your payments once in a while, whereas the state will automatically record the delinquency and charge interest.

Tracking Child Support Payments

Whether you are paying or receiving child support, you need to document the payments. Even state agencies can make mistakes.

If you are paying child support, make sure you record every payment made. Missed payments and payments you made but can't prove if your spouse challenges them can result in a judgment against you and suspension of your driver's license. If you are making payments directly to the custodial parent, you may wish to ask him or her to sign a receipt acknowledging each one. Use the sample Child Support Receipts and obtain one for each payment. Store the signed receipts in the accordion folder pocket labeled "Child Support Receipts." If you are making payments to a child support collection unit, record each payment on the Child Support Payment Log at the end of this chapter.

The custodial parent can also use the Child Support Payment Log to track both payments that were received and those that were missed. The log will come in handy if the noncustodial parent claims to have made a payment in cash that was never received. If payment is made through your state, you can compare your log to the statements or online account created by the state. If you are the custodial parent, never sign a receipt for payment without first receiving the payment. If payments are to be made through the state, do not accept payment from your spouse directly, as this will complicate the process.

Due Dates

When you first start to pay or receive child support, it's a good idea to include payment due dates on your calendar. You probably won't need to do this after a few months, but in the beginning, it is helpful to write it down so you don't miss a payment or can recognize when your spouse is late with a payment.

Nonpayment

Failure to pay child support can result in a judgment against the payer, revocation of driver's and other licenses, and even jail time. If you don't pay, you'll owe not only the arrears but also the interest, and you'll undoubtedly rack up legal bills in the process. Failure to pay child support can also have a long-term impact on your relationship with your child, who will someday be old enough to get the facts and may feel betrayed.

110

Adjusting Child Support

As time goes by, you may need to adjust or modify the amount of child support due to changes in circumstances. If you are the payer and you lose your job or have a serious illness that impacts your ability to work, you might need to ask for a reduction. Additionally, if the parent receiving child support from you has an increase in household income, you can ask that the amount you pay be reduced.

If you are the parent receiving child support and you know the other parent has received a pay raise or has remarried and had an increase in household income, or if you have experienced a decrease in your household income, you might want to ask for more child support. Additionally, if your child's situation has changed (a drastic change in health, for example), you can also have child support modified upward. To make these adjustments, you'll need to contact your attorney and return to court. You'll also need to document your reasons for requesting a change. If child support is being paid through your state child support collection agency, the agency may automatically adjust the amount every few years for inflation. This is referred to as a cost of living adjustment (COLA). It is possible to have a clause about this inserted into direct-pay child support agreements as well.

CHILDREN'S EXPENSES

List monthly amounts. For expenses that are less frequent than once a month, determine the yearly amount and then divide by twelve to reach the monthly cost.

Day care _____

Tuition _____

School or day care registration fees _____

Babysitting/nanny _____

After-school day care _____

School books _____

School supplies _____

School lunches, snacks, and meals _____

School photos _____

Field trip expenses _____

Donations requested by the school _____

School event fees _____

Music/vocal lessons _____

Musical instrument rental or payment _____

Music supplies _____

Music competition fees _____

Band/orchestra/chorus uniforms or costumes _____

Music group photos _____

Other lesson fees _____

Other lesson supplies _____

Sports uniforms _____

Sports supplies and equipment _____

Sports fees _____

Sports photos _____

Dance lessons _____

Dance supplies _____

Dance costumes _____

Dance competition fees _____

Dance photos _____

Costs for other lessons and supplies _____

Girl or Boy Scout fees _____

Scout uniforms _____

Scout supplies _____

Scout photos _____

Extracurricular club membership fees _____

Extracurricular club supplies _____

Extracurricular photos _____

Other club fees _____

Other club supplies _____

Other group photos _____

Camp fees _____

Camp supplies _____

Tutoring _____

Approximate mileage per month for children's transportation _____

Children's transportation fees (such as teen's car) _____

Monthly children's clothing/footwear costs _____

Monthly children's hobby costs _____

Children's pets' costs _____

Birthday/holiday gifts _____

Gifts for children to take to birthday parties _____

Children's Internet access _____

Children's computer costs _____

Children's computer supplies _____

Children's cell phone and data costs _____

Entertainment _____

Toys and books _____

Regular medical/dental/orthodontic/vision/mental health
supplies and services _____

Backpacks, bags, lunch boxes, purses _____

Allowance _____

Onetime expenses, such as yearbooks, school rings, field trips,
teacher gifts, school donations, school T-shirts, school photos,
school dances, prom, graduation costs (divide by twelve) _____

TOTAL _____

CHILDREN'S UNINSURED HEALTH EXPENSES

Create one of these forms for each month of the year.

Children's Uninsured Health Expenses for the Month of _____

Child	Date	Description	Cost	Date Payment Received

Prepare a receipt for each payment.

Child Support Receipt

I received $_____ from _____ on _____ [date]

for the period of _____ to _____ as child support.

_____

[signature]

Child Support Receipt

I received $_____ from _____ on _____ [date]

for the period of _____ to _____ as child support.

_____

[signature]

Child Support Receipt

I received $_____ from _____ on _____ [date]

for the period of _____ to _____ as child support.

_____

[signature]

Child Support Receipt

I received $_____ from _____ on _____ [date]

for the period of _____ to _____ as child support.

_____

[signature]

CHILD SUPPORT PAYMENT LOG

Date	Check Number	Amount	Payment Period	Check if Unpaid

13

Alimony

Alimony, or spousal support, is often awarded to help one spouse become self-supporting. It can also be used as a kind of property settlement; instead of a specified amount of cash or property distributed at the time of the divorce, a spouse receives regular alimony payments for a certain period of time. Alimony is rarely used as a way to punish a spouse for things he or she did that led to the end of the marriage.

Some people mistakenly think that one spouse automatically gets alimony in every divorce case. In fact, it's not the norm. For example, in some states, alimony is generally awarded only if a spouse needs assistance while going back to school or looking for a job. Talk to your attorney about the alimony laws in your state and find out when and how it is normally awarded.

How Alimony Is Awarded

When deciding if there will be alimony and how much will be awarded, judges usually consider these factors:

- **The length of the marriage.** Usually, the longer the marriage, the longer the payment period.
- **The health of the spouses.** If one spouse has a disability or an illness, he or she will more likely need financial support.
- **The parties' incomes and property.** If your spouse earns a lot more than you do or owns a lot of valuable separate property, this can increase your chances of being eligible for alimony.
- **The parties' earning abilities and skills.** This would be a factor if one spouse stayed home with the children and had no income but had a medical degree and thus the potential to earn a decent living if he or she went back to work.

- **Lost earnings.** One spouse might have lost years of earnings because he or she stayed home to care for children.
- **Contributions each spouse made to the marriage financially and emotionally.** These would include nurturing children or supporting a spouse who earned a degree or started a business.
- **With which parent the children live.** This impacts the custodial parent's financial situation and needs.
- **Whether either spouse has wasted marital assets.** Wasting assets means you've spent them, given them away, or mismanaged them. Often this is done with the intention of keeping them from the other spouse.
- **How the parties treated marital assets during the divorce.** If one spouse destroyed property or exhibited a careless attitude about conserving property, it will be considered.
- **Bad behavior by either party.** This includes emotional or physical abuse.

In many states, the rule of thumb is that alimony is granted for one-third of the length of the marriage, so a nine-year marriage would have a three-year alimony payment, but it can also be paid in one lump sum. Lifetime alimony can be awarded when a spouse is ill, elderly, or disabled, or a lifetime amount could be awarded as a onetime payment. An alimony lump-sum payout is similar to a property settlement, but the tax consequences are different. Alimony is tax deductible for the person paying it and taxable income for the person receiving it, so a big lump-sum alimony payment has important tax consequences. Property settlements, on the other hand, are not taxable or tax deductible. One spouse can also be ordered to pay the other's household expenses as a type of alimony.

Seeking Alimony

If you are seeking alimony, you want to minimize your own income, maximize your spouse's income, highlight the many unselfish contributions you made to the marriage, and show how your contributions limited your ability to earn an income. You also want to show that your spouse has depleted (used up or wasted) marital assets. Overall, you want to portray yourself as responsible and needy and your spouse as selfish, rich, and irresponsible. You can receive temporary spousal support during the divorce, as well as alimony after the case is decided.

Alimony Rules and Regulations

Any alimony or spousal support money you receive is taxable income and must be reported. Because alimony has tax consequences, and because the spouse paying alimony can be subject to contempt of court orders for failing to meet his or her obligation, it is imperative to keep careful records of alimony paid or received.

Talk with your attorney about balancing alimony with child support. If you are the spouse paying alimony and child support, it is more advantageous to pay a higher amount in alimony, because it is tax deductible and often ends sooner than child support obligations. If you are the spouse receiving alimony and child support, it is more advantageous to receive a higher child support payment, because you don't have to report it as income, and it will probably have a longer duration than alimony. Alimony ends upon the death of either spouse and also usually ends if the spouse receiving it remarries.

If you are seeking alimony, consult the list of considerations for how alimony is awarded at the beginning of this chapter to build your case. Complete the Alimony Worksheet at the end of this chapter and share it with your attorney when you discuss alimony.

Tracking Alimony

Unlike child support, alimony is always paid directly to the other spouse—the state will not collect and manage alimony payments. If you are the spouse paying alimony, always get a receipt. A cashed check is sufficient if you write "alimony" and the period it covers in the memo section. But since most banks no longer return checks without specific requests (although many allow you to access images of them online), it may be simpler to have your spouse sign a receipt for each payment. It is a good idea to pay by check whenever possible so that you have two kinds of proof of payment—the canceled check and the signed receipt. Receipts are necessary if you want to deduct alimony payments from your taxes or if you have to prove to a court that you paid in full. Use the Alimony Receipts and store them in the "Alimony Receipts" pocket in your accordion folder.

If you are the spouse receiving alimony, you need to track payments so that you have proof of a missed payment and accurate records to use when reporting alimony on your income taxes. Use the Alimony Payment Log to record this information.

Medical Insurance

If you are covered by your spouse's medical insurance policy at the time of your divorce, you are eligible to continue your coverage on the policy through a federal law called COBRA (the Consolidated Omnibus Budget Reconciliation Act). COBRA allows you to continue your coverage for up to thirty-six months, but you have to pay for it yourself (payments are made to your spouse's employer and are equal to the full amount of both employer and employee contributions to the premium for one person) unless the court orders your spouse to pay it as a form of alimony or property settlement. After this time, you will need to obtain your own policy. Note that even if your spouse changes jobs, you are still able to continue your COBRA coverage through the employer. You will want to talk to the human resources department to discuss the amount of the payment and how and when you need to pay the monthly premiums.

If your spouse is in the military, you are entitled to continue your medical benefits if you have been married more than ten years and if ten or more years of your marriage occurred during your spouse's military service. If you've been married more than twenty years (and twenty years of the marriage were during the military service), you can get extended benefits. If you do not qualify for benefits, you can pay for the Continued Health Care Benefit Program (CHCBP).

ALIMONY WORKSHEET ▶

Length of your marriage _____

Describe your health, noting any disabilities, limitations, or serious health concerns.

_____
_____
_____
_____

Describe differences in your and your spouse's income and property ownership.

_____
_____
_____
_____

Describe your earning ability and skills. What kind of education or training do you need to improve these? How long will it take to do so, and how much will it cost? If you are unemployed, what kind of training or education do you need to become employable?

_____
_____
_____
_____

Describe anything you did during your marriage that decreased your earning potential (such as staying home with the children or giving up a job to move with your spouse). For how long did you do this? What position did you leave to do so? What did it pay?

_____
_____
_____
_____

continued ▶

Describe the contributions you made to the marriage, both financially and emotionally (time and energy you devoted to caring for the children, advancing your spouse's career, and so on).

_____

_____

_____

_____

With whom will the children be living after the marriage? _____

Has your spouse wasted or used up marital assets? Explain how he or she did so, and provide a value and description of the assets.

_____

_____

_____

_____

Describe anything your spouse did during the marriage that decreased the value of any marital assets.

_____

_____

_____

_____

Describe any abuse or unpleasantness your spouse has shown you.

_____

_____

_____

_____

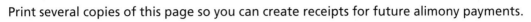

Print several copies of this page so you can create receipts for future alimony payments.

Alimony Receipt

I received $_____ from _____ on _____ [date]

for the period of _____ to _____ as alimony.

_____

[signature]

Alimony Receipt

I received $_____ from _____ on _____ [date]

for the period of _____ to _____ as alimony.

_____

[signature]

Alimony Receipt

I received $_____ from _____ on _____ [date]

for the period of _____ to _____ as alimony.

_____

[signature]

Alimony Receipt

I received $_____ from _____ on _____ [date]

for the period of _____ to _____ as alimony.

_____

[signature]

ALIMONY PAYMENT LOG

Date	Check Number	Amount	Payment Period	Check if Unpaid

14

Custody and Visitation

If your divorce involves a dispute over custody and visitation, you're probably very concerned about what the court will decide. If you have children, this is probably the key issue in your divorce.

Temporary Custody

In most cases, the court will first issue a temporary order of custody, deciding where the children will live and how they will split their time with the parents while the case is ongoing. For this order, the court usually seeks to preserve the status quo, meaning that most of the time the children will remain where they are, and whatever arrangement you and your spouse have worked out will remain in place. If temporary custody and visitation are hotly disputed, you will have a hearing (a short trial) where your attorneys will provide evidence and the judge will make a decision. Temporary custody orders are exactly that—temporary. However, judges do tend to make them into permanent orders, so make sure you give your attorney all relevant information before a temporary custody order is issued.

Understanding Custody

Custody decisions are based on what is in the best interests of the children—what overall parenting arrangement will work best for them and allow them to have normal and happy lives. Courts believe that it is important for children to have both parents in their lives whenever possible, and many states have a preference for joint custody. The judge will look for a solution that will let your children spend time with both of you in a way that makes the most sense for everyone involved.

The time during which your divorce is pending is the most crucial point for custody cases. During this time, everything you and your spouse do is under the watchful eye of the court. The way you parented before the divorce is important, but it isn't as obvious and immediate to the judge. The way you and your spouse spend time with your children during the divorce will be what the court gives the most consideration to, simply because there will be the most evidence available about it.

While your case is ongoing, it is essential that you keep good records of how your children divide their time, as well as any parenting problems and concerns that arise. It is important that you create a record that reflects your point of view. If you are the parent who has temporary residential custody of the children, be sure to record all the time you spend with them as well as the times your spouse misses visitations. If you are the parent with temporary visitation, you want to create a record that shows how you maximized your time with your children and document anything your spouse does to interfere with that.

Tips for Avoiding a Custody Trial

Custody trials can be painful, particularly for the children. They can also be expensive, so it's in your best interest to do everything you can to avoid one. Consider these steps:

- Think long and hard about what kind of arrangement would work best for your children.
- Consider what kind of arrangement feels natural to you.
- Remember that your children have two parents and must have time with both.
- Keep in mind that there is a big difference between being a good spouse and being a good parent. You may not think much of your spouse as a partner, but that doesn't mean he or she isn't a good parent.
- Try not to get caught up in the words that designate how the time is divided—*custody*, *visitation*, *residential parent*, and *custodial parent* sound unpleasant. Focus instead on sharing time.
- Don't ask your children to make a decision or indicate a preference. Make a concerted effort to keep them out of this discussion. Children need to know they have no control over this and anything that happens is not their fault.
- Take an honest look at each parent's schedule and lifestyle, and think about how the children fit into that schedule. Someone who works a night shift is going to have a hard time being the residential parent.
- Make it clear to the other parent that you want him or her to be an important part of the children's lives. This is what they need.
- Try to talk with your spouse about what kind of arrangement will work best for the children. See if you can reach an agreement together.
- Look at parenting time as something that belongs to your children, not to you and your spouse.

- Think not in terms of who gets the most time, but in terms of what time-sharing arrangement will work best for your children, with emphasis on not disrupting their lifestyle.
- Consider seeing a mediator if you are not able to agree about custody.

Decisions About Custody and Visitation

The first impulse in a divorce is often to grab what you can and run, even with respect to the children. When it comes to custody, you probably feel as though you want to maximize your time with your kids while minimizing your spouse's time. Although you do want the court to create a schedule that gives you as much time as you need with your children, you also have to think about what's best for them. They need a balanced, stable, and relatively stress-free life, and in most cases, they need time with both parents.

Before the divorce or separation, your children lived in a home with two parents and had contact with both of them. Now that you and your spouse live in two separate homes, your children should continue receiving the emotional and financial support they have grown accustomed to.

Children also need a sense of normalcy and a schedule. How rigid this schedule needs to be depends on their age. In general, the older the child, the more flexible you can be. Children need a schedule they can rely on, so it's important to develop and follow a plan that allows your children time with each of you on a regular basis. At the same time, parents need to be flexible to accommodate each other's schedules and their children's schedules and needs.

This chapter helps you create an accurate record of how you and your spouse are sharing your time with your children during the divorce. As you read, keep in mind that the whole point of a parenting plan is to allow children to spend time with both parents. Instead of trying to cut your spouse out of the picture, think about persuading the court to create a schedule that allows your child time with each of you. You may have different viewpoints about what is sensible and fair, but it's important that you approach the issue with that mindset.

Some states no longer use the words *custody* and *visitation* because they have negative connotations. After all, no one truly owns a child, and a parent doesn't visit with a child. The prevailing thinking in the children's rights field is to refer to *parenting plans*, *access*, or *parenting time*. Most people, however, still think in terms of custody and visitation. The most important thing you want to look at is how the plan divides time between parents and whether you have decision-making power (for health, school, and religion, among other things).

ABUSE OR NEGLECT

If you are in a situation where you have serious concerns about your spouse's ability to care for your children, or there is a history of abuse or neglect, it is important that you let your attorney know about this immediately. If there has been any involvement with your state's social services department (sometimes called the Department of Children and Families), you need to provide your attorney with any documentation you have about prior investigations.

Gather Evidence to Help Your Attorney

Even if you're fine with your ex spending time with your children, you may want to be the custodial parent. You may also feel strongly about being named as the sole custodian, meaning you have complete control over all decisions concerning your kids. Whatever kind of arrangement you're looking for, there are some things you can do that will help your attorney with your case.

Your camera phone is your best friend when it comes to documenting evidence. A picture is definitely worth a thousand words, and many a custody case has turned on photographic evidence. Use your camera phone to record anything that would make a court concerned about your spouse's care of your child. Is your ex's house a disaster? Snap a few quick photos or shoot a quick video. Is your child returned to you with horrific diaper rash, dirty clothes, or bruises? Photograph it. Did your ex fail to give your child necessary medication? Take photos before and after the visit to document that no meds have been used.

Print out all e-mails and texts from your ex that indicate anything worrisome, such as messages that she doesn't care if she's late for pickup, that your child is a brat, or that he never wanted to be a parent. Expand your thinking to social media as well. Is your ex supposed to be with your child on Saturday night but posted photos of himself drinking or partying on that night? Take screenshots and give this evidence to your attorney. Does your ex post negative things about your child on social media? Save these as well. Your ex might even discuss drug or alcohol use on social media, and this will be of concern to the court.

Save all voice mails from your ex that are in any way negative. Do *not* quiz your children about what happens while they are with the other parent. You need to be very careful that you do not put your children in the middle or ask them to "tell" on the other parent.

It may be tempting to use your cell phone to videotape or audio record your spouse. Before you do something like this, you must talk to your attorney. It is illegal in some states to record another person without his or her permission.

You should be able to access your cell phone records on your online account, and here you can print out call logs showing all calls as well as duration, which can be useful for your attorney if you are trying to show that your ex never called to reschedule a visit or that he or she has called excessively. You can also view logs of text messages online but not the content of the messages, which is why it is important to preserve all texts from your spouse on your phone.

Chapter 15 discusses the types of witnesses that may be useful for your custody trial.

Creating an Accurate Visitation Record

As discussed earlier, while your case is pending, you will probably have a temporary order from the court describing a basic parenting schedule. In cases where the parents are able to work things out, a court will simply order "visitation at times as agreed," which gives you the flexibility to create a schedule that fits both of your needs. Whether you agree on a schedule or not, it's important that you keep an accurate record of when you each spend time with your children. Record all actual parenting time on your calendar so you can present your attorney with an accurate log of how time has been divided.

When you get the temporary order describing when visitation is going to occur, record the schedule on your calendar. If the children are going to reside primarily with you, mark the times that they are to be with your spouse. If you are the parent with temporary visitation, mark the times that are yours to spend with the children, then be sure you go back to your calendar and mark down what actually happens—your ex late bringing the kids home, he or she refused visitation, and so on. It can be helpful to keep a calendar or document on your phone where you can quickly record times when the event happens, so you don't have to try to remember what happened later.

Some parents create a separate visitation calendar that shows each parent's time in a different color for easy visual processing. This calendar can show you at a glance where the children will be, and it is easy for young children to understand (blue days are Mom's, red days are Dad's).

Parenting Time Issues to Record

It is important to keep some records so you have proof of problems with parenting time.

Late Pickups or Drop-Offs
Pay attention to pickup and drop-off times. If your spouse is late picking up the children for his or her visit or bringing the children to you for your visit, make a note of it. Five minutes isn't important, but a half hour is, particularly if it becomes a pattern. It may seem picky to write down actual pickup and drop-off times, but single instances can develop into larger patterns, and if you keep track of them, you will have an accurate record of the problem.

Missed Visits
If your spouse forgets or cancels a scheduled visit with your children, note it on your calendar. Everyone forgets things once in a while, and situations arise that require us to cancel plans, but if this becomes a habit, you'll want a clear record of when and how often it happened. Children need routine, and if your spouse can't stick to one, you might use this information to persuade the court to cut back on his or her visitation time. On the flip side, if a parent doesn't spend time with the children, you can't force him or her to use visitation time, but you must continue to make that time available to him or her or you will violate the court order. You can point out how upsetting it is for the children to be left waiting and encourage him or her to show up as planned. Missed visits can be powerful evidence to refute your ex's request for custody.

If you are the parent with visitation time and your spouse is canceling your visits, forgetting about them, or simply not allowing you access to the children, make sure you record these problems and discuss them with your attorney. Interference with visitation can be the basis for a change in custody. You don't want to encounter a situation where your spouse tells the court you're the one who didn't show up, so write down the times you went to pick up your children and note what happened.

Changes in Visitation

Some change to the parenting schedule is inevitable. You, your spouse, and your children all have busy lives, and things are bound to pop up now and then. If you agree to changes, make sure you record them on your calendar, and try to distribute the visits so that everyone gets a fair amount of time. For example, it's common for parents to alternate weekends:

Weekend 1: Parent A
Weekend 2: Parent B
Weekend 3: Parent A
Weekend 4: Parent B
Weekend 5: Parent A

When weekends are switched, the result can seem unfair. The visitation schedule could end up like this if the parents swapped Weekend 2 with Weekend 5:

Weekend 1: Parent A
Weekend 2: Parent A
Weekend 3: Parent A
Weekend 4: Parent B
Weekend 5: Parent B

The revised format doesn't feel as fair as the original one, but it still gives each parent the same amount of time. Writing it down can show everyone that time is still fairly distributed.

When you agree to a change in visitation, record it on your calendar. Note the date it was changed from and which of you requested the change. If you get to a point where your spouse is requesting constant changes, you'll be able to show this pattern to the court. Constant changes can be upsetting to children, especially when they are first adjusting to a visitation schedule and the concept of divorce. Constant changes are also a sign that the current visitation plan is not working and may need to be modified.

Keep all e-mails and texts about changes to the schedule. This can prove who requested them if there is ever an issue and will also show who is being flexible and cooperative and who is not. It can also demonstrate excessive requests for changes, which are of interest to the court.

You may want to download an app that will help you keep track of your visitation schedule (see the Resources section at the end of this book for specific apps).

Documenting Shared Custody

In most situations, judges identify one home that will be the children's primary residence and set up times when the nonresidential parent will have access. But in some situations, the court divides the children's time equally between the parents, giving neither actual residential custody. This arrangement is called joint, shared, or split custody. It might involve children spending one week with one parent, the next week with the other, or half the week with one parent and half with the other. On rare occasions, time may be divided monthly.

If you and your spouse have shared custody, you'll want to keep a clear record of where your children will be each day for your own scheduling reasons and to create documentation for the court. Record changes, tardiness, and missed days on the calendar. Share your custody documentation with your attorney. You may also want to share it with the law guardian (also called the guardian *ad litem*, the attorney representing the children), if your attorney feels it would be helpful.

Monitoring Your Children's Responses to Visitation

Throughout your divorce, pay attention to how your children react to the parenting access schedule. Keep in mind that a new schedule, a divorce, and one parent moving into a new home are huge changes for children. Expect them to have trouble getting used to it all. Most parents are worried by the way their children react to divorce, and sometimes the knee-jerk response is to blame the other parent. In fact, it is normal for your kids to have some difficulty adjusting (think about the trouble *you're* having adjusting, and realize your children are going through the same situation).

While it's important to keep an eye on your children's reactions, don't read too much into them. For example, if a child cries or screams each time he or she goes with the other parent, your first inclination might be that your spouse is doing something to cause this. Most of the time, the child is just reacting to the stress and newness of the situation and to the emotions of his or her parents.

Sometimes the problem goes deeper. Sometimes an arrangement just isn't working for a child. The emphasis in these situations should be on finding solutions, not pointing fingers. Some children, for example, have a hard time with transitions (going from one parent to the other). Changing the time or location of the transition can help a lot in these situations. Other kids might resent having to miss soccer practice or Girl Scouts to go with a parent for a scheduled visit. Try to adjust the schedule around your children's needs. If your spouse is not cooperating, you need to document that for the court.

What seems like a crisis to you and your children may not seem so serious to a judge who has seen hundreds of children react to divorce. They don't have an easy time of it, but most children do adjust eventually. The court is not going to change custody or alter visitation simply because your child is having a hard time getting used to the situation. You need to present persistent, ongoing reactions that clearly point to a problem. Keep detailed notes in the Children's Reactions Log at the end of this chapter. You'll want to share this with your attorney and perhaps with the law guardian/guardian *ad litem*, if your attorney agrees.

If your children are having trouble handling the situation, a therapist can help them work through the confused emotions associated with the divorce and all the changes it brings. A therapist can also be called to testify, if necessary, and provide a professional opinion about the custody situation. Some cases involve formal custody evaluations where a mental health professional talks to both parents and the children and makes a recommendation. Talk to your attorney about whether this would be helpful in your case.

KNOW WHERE YOUR CHILDREN ARE

If your children are old enough to have a smartphone (and most kids are by middle school), consider installing an app like Find My Friends on their phones. This allows you to locate where they and their phones are at any time. If you have concerns about where your spouse is taking your children during visitation, this app can give you great peace of mind. It can also be used as evidence. If you suspect your spouse leaves the kids at his or her parents' house for every weekend visitation, this will show you the truth.

Children's Preferences

Courts pay attention to children's preferences about where they want to live when the children are in their preteen or teenage years, but children do *not* get to decide. What a child wants may not be what is in his or her best interest, so the court will always weigh all the evidence before making a decision. Although they may have strong preferences, younger children aren't given as much say. A child's maturity level is a factor in custody decisions (the older the child, the more weight his or her opinion has).

As mentioned in earlier chapters, no matter what your children's ages, they will probably have a law guardian, or guardian *ad litem*—an attorney appointed by the court to represent them throughout the case. This lawyer meets with the children to find out how they feel about living arrangements and schedules and may also offer an opinion about how the case should be decided.

Parents should not try to influence their children's opinions. Don't panic if a young child doesn't want to live with you. The judge and the law guardian are not going to base their decisions on what he or she says. They understand that children go through different phases while coping with divorce, and this involves frequent switching of loyalties. The court will take into consideration the opinions of teenagers who have a distinct preference about where they want to live, so listen to them and treat them with respect, even if you don't agree.

Grandparent Visitation

132

More and more courts are recognizing the importance of grandparents in a child's life. Although grandparents' rights are limited in some states, some courts will include provisions for grandparents to have access to their grandchildren in a divorce decree or separate visitation order; however, this is common only when the grandparents have an established relationship with the child. Usually the noncustodial parent's parents are the ones who are given formal access to the children, since it is assumed that the custodial parent can ensure that his or her own parents have access. For example, if Mom has residential custody and Dad has visitation, the children will probably see Mom's parents on a regular basis, since they will spend most of their time with Mom. However, because Dad's time is limited, his parents might want the court to give them their own designated time with the kids. If the noncustodial parent has limited access to the children, the court will want to make sure that the grandparents on that side of the family have access.

If you oppose access by your in-laws, you'll need to document why you don't want your children to spend time with them. Keep notes about your children's visits with them, and list any problems that have occurred. You'll want to document late pickups or drop-offs, as well as missed visits. Use the Grandparent Visitation Log to record that information.

If you're arguing for your own parents to have access to your children, keep notes that record how they spend time with the children, how the children enjoy their time with their grandparents, and how your spouse tries to interfere with or prevent the visits. It can also be helpful to take photos of your children with their grandparents.

CHILDREN'S REACTIONS LOG

Date	Description

GRANDPARENT VISITATION LOG ▶

Name of grandparents _____

List the reasons you are opposed to visitation with these grandparents.

_____
_____
_____
_____
_____
_____

Create a log of problems that occur with grandparent visitation.

Date	Description

15

Witnesses and Evidence

Witnesses can be one of the most helpful types of evidence presented in a divorce, particularly with regard to custody. A custody decision is based on many subjective factors, such as a judge's perception, values, and opinions. Because judges in most states base their decisions on what is in the best interests of the children, and because witnesses are considered less biased than the parents, the court's decision will rely heavily on witnesses and their credibility. Witnesses can literally make or break your bid for custody. They can also provide important information for other parts of your case that don't deal with custody.

This chapter assists you in finding witnesses and summarizing how they can help your case. It also offers advice on preparing your own testimony. Doing these things yourself will reduce the time your attorney needs to spend interviewing potential witnesses and preparing for the case.

Why You Need Witnesses

Witnesses present facts, opinions, and observations to the judge. If you testify that your spouse hit your child or withdrew all the money from your savings account, the judge will certainly consider your statement. However, if your neighbor testifies that she saw your spouse hit your child for spilling a cup of juice on the patio or that she heard your spouse talk about withdrawing all the money from your savings account, the judge will give more credence to her testimony because she is perceived as having no vested interest in the case.

Witnesses are also important because trials can be boring. A sheaf of papers may give the judge enough evidence to support your position, but live testimony is much more compelling, and the judge is more likely to pay attention to it. Lawyers can do more

137

with witnesses than they can with documents. Careful questioning can discredit many witnesses or make certain facts stand out. If the judge likes your witnesses, he or she is apt to like you. Remember, though, that the more witnesses your attorney presents, the longer the trial will last and the larger your legal bill will be. It's important that you and your attorney come up with enough witnesses to prove your case but not so many that the proceedings become redundant and expensive.

Types of Witnesses to Find

Think about everything you are asking for in your divorce. Then consider the people who will be able to offer facts or opinions that will convince the judge to give you what you want.

There are two types of witnesses: character witnesses and fact-based witnesses. Character witnesses are those who can say generally good things about you (or bad things about your spouse) and provide an overall description of what you are like as a person. This kind of witness gives information about overall character and personality. Character witnesses are important when custody is being determined, because they can affect the judge's impression of the parties. They should be people who know you well and have known you for a long time, if possible. The same is true for character witnesses who point out negative qualities in your spouse.

Fact-based witnesses are those who can testify about things they know or saw. They are useful for any issue in a divorce.

Your lawyer probably will not call all of the witnesses you've gathered, but it is helpful for him or her to have a list to work from. You want to give your attorney choices, because some witnesses will perform better than others. Some people may be able to provide background information or documents that can be entered into evidence even if they don't testify, so don't leave them off your list.

Witness Characteristics

The best witnesses are those who can be objective—or at least *appear* objective. While your mother and brother may be able to testify about what a fantastic parent you are, the judge will understand that they have a vested interest in the case. If a close relative is the only one who can provide certain information, it is better to have the relative testify than no one at all, but the final call on this will be up to your lawyer.

You want your witnesses to be upstanding citizens, whenever possible. Witnesses who are employed, have a stable lifestyle, have no criminal history or substance abuse problems, and have been decent people for much of their lives will do you the most good. You don't need Mary Poppins, but you want to avoid someone your spouse's attorney can turn the tables on during cross-examination. Don't worry about trying to find witnesses who are perfect—your attorney will be able to work around their imperfections. Focus on coming up with credible people who can provide the best information to help your case.

138

Hearsay

Witnesses must have personal knowledge of the things they testify to. The hearsay rule, which prohibits people from testifying about things they do not have personal knowledge or experience with, must be taken into consideration when choosing your witnesses. For example, a witness can testify that he saw your spouse win $20,000 at a casino, but he cannot testify that his coworker saw this and then told him about it. He can't be sure it's true if he didn't see it himself. If you doubt whether a witness will be able to testify about something, include him or her on your list and let your attorney decide.

Subject Matter for Witness Testimony

The following are examples of the types of witnesses you may need for the various issues in your divorce. Your attorney will make the final call on which ones will be most helpful.

Alimony
- Professionals such as office managers, human resources employees, or business partners who can provide proof of your or your spouse's income, assets, and expenses.
- Anyone who can testify about unreported income your spouse is earning. If your spouse is being paid in cash, is doing consulting or odd jobs on the side, or is regularly earning cash at a flea market or online, and someone has firsthand knowledge of this, you want that witness.
- People who have direct knowledge of your ex's "bad behavior," such as infidelity. Anyone with firsthand knowledge of domestic violence is another important witness.
- Professionals who can support or refute career or educational needs and expenses after divorce for the spouse who is seeking alimony (for example, an employer or a college career counselor).

Child Support
- People who can provide proof of your or your spouse's income or assets or who have information about unreported income, such as office managers, human resources personnel, business partners, bank personnel, or anyone who has knowledge of under-the-table cash payments.
- Experts who can support or refute testimony about your children's special needs, such as physical therapists, physicians, mental health therapists, or teachers.

Property and Debt Division
- An expert who can value a business or license.
- Family members, business associates, and others who have information about assets that your spouse may have hidden or stolen.
- People, such as family members or friends, from whom you or your ex have borrowed money when there is no documentary proof of the loan.

- Experts who can value real estate, jewelry, or any special collections or special items of value.

Custody

- Day care providers. They can testify about how timely your ex is with pickups and drop-offs, as well as what condition the children are in when dropped off.
- Teachers. They can be helpful witnesses to show how involved you are as a parent, but they can also testify that they've never met the other parent, that the other parent has forgotten to pack a lunch, or that your children's homework noticeably suffers from visitation nights. They can also testify about behavioral changes that regularly occur right before or after visitation.
- Neighbors. They have seen your family before, during, and after separation and are in a good position to talk about what a great parent you are and problems they see in your spouse's parenting.
- Relatives. They can be useful witnesses but are usually considered to be biased. However, if you know one of your ex's relatives saw something that is damaging to your ex's case, let your attorney know. That person can be subpoenaed and forced to testify.
- Friends. Like relatives, they are generally considered biased, but sometimes it can be useful to have them talk about your parenting skills, as well as about anything damaging to your spouse.
- Therapists, psychologists, or doctors who can discuss your children's special needs, parental involvement, and family dynamics.
- Therapists or psychologists who can evaluate your and your spouse's parenting abilities.

Reason for Divorce

- For contested grounds (which are rare), witnesses who have knowledge of the reasons behind the breakup of the marriage.

Your lawyer will want to use documents to prove many financial facts, because it is faster and less expensive than bringing in live witnesses. Why have your bank manager testify about how much money is in your savings account when you can prove it with bank records? However, it is a good idea to include witnesses on your list who can back up the evidence in the documents in case of a dispute. The classic example of a witness who can back up the information in documentary evidence is the office manager or someone from your spouse's place of employment who can testify about the availability of overtime, your spouse's history of accepting it, and the fact that he or she has cut back on overtime since the divorce proceedings began—a tactic used to reduce income so that child support and alimony will be lower.

Preparing a Witness List

Once you have thought about the kind of information you need and the people who can provide it, complete the List of Possible Witnesses form at the end of this chapter. Then

WHAT NOT TO DO WHEN YOU TESTIFY

When you testify, always tell the truth, no matter how damaging it is. It is tempting to try to hide things or misrepresent them to make things look better, but doing so usually makes you look dishonest in the end. You should discuss anything that could be used against you with your attorney in advance so you have a strategy for how to approach it.

- Don't answer a question you don't understand. If you don't understand it, say so!
- Don't act hostile, angry, resentful, or suspicious while you are testifying. You may experience these emotions, but you should try not to let them show.
- Avoid confronting the other attorney. Your attorney will handle anything that is inappropriate.
- When you are being cross-examined, answer the questions truthfully but as briefly as possible. Don't give a lot of details. If you are asked what kind of car you drive, say, "A Dodge," instead of giving the year, make, and model.
- Don't use terms that are absolute like "I never," "I always," or "That's everything I remember." No matter how sure you are, you might remember something later that contradicts this.
- If the attorney cross-examining you tries to summarize something that happened and then asks you if it is true, you do not have to answer yes or no. Point out what is true and what isn't.
- As tempting as it might be, don't talk to your ex while you are on the stand or respond to anything he or she says while on the stand.
- Don't be shy. Make eye contact with the attorney talking to you. Make eye contact with the judge if he or she speaks to you.

fill out a Witness Worksheet for each person. Fill in the contact information at the top of the sheet, write in the facts the witness can share, and indicate whether he or she can offer character evidence about you. Make note of important events he or she has witnessed. Take a few days to complete these worksheets, and jot down points as they come to mind. Although you want to organize your information logically, it's more important to get it all down than to have it in perfect form. Your attorney will create his or her own notes anyway.

It's permissible to talk to the people you put on your witness list to see if they remember what you remember. Tell them you want them to testify and that they may need to speak with your attorney if they can be used as witnesses, but don't try to influence what they will say. You can add people to your list who are not willing to testify if you believe they have information that will help your case. You should not try to talk to these people about what they know, because they could change their story or alert your spouse. Your attorney can subpoena them and require them to testify. Make sure you discuss these witnesses thoroughly with your attorney, because they may be upset that they have been subpoenaed. Never promise anyone anything in exchange for his or her testimony, and do not threaten anyone who refuses to testify or testifies against you.

Some witnesses may have documents or other types of evidence that can help your case. It is best if they give these items directly to your attorney, but if a witness insists on giving something to you, accept it and pass it along.

Being Your Own Witness

Most parties in a divorce case will usually end up testifying themselves. After all, you are the one who has the most information about your situation. When you testify, your job will be to answer the questions you are asked, first by your attorney and then by your spouse's attorney (and sometimes by the law guardian/guardian *ad litem* for your children if custody is an issue). Note that the judge may ask you a few questions as well. Your attorney will help you prepare your testimony, but it is important to be truthful and to report things accurately. You will usually start with basic information such as your name, age, employer, income, and where you live.

To prepare yourself to testify, create a comprehensive list of events and facts that are essential to your case and about which you can provide information. Even if you have other witnesses, your attorney should have a complete list of what you can testify about. He or she will decide if each item is relevant and, if so, how to present the information. Use the Notes for Your Testimony worksheet to record the items you think you can testify about. Work on it over a few days, jotting things down as they occur to you. Try to group your thoughts under the categories on the worksheet. If you're not sure where something goes, place it under "Other." Don't try to include all the details—just cover the key points. You can discuss the details with your attorney. Once you have written down everything you can remember, read it over and cross out things about which you do not have firsthand knowledge. This list will give your attorney an outline to use in preparing you for questioning. Things you might include on your list:

- Abuse by your spouse
- Hidden income or earnings by your spouse during the marriage
- Your plans to return to school or work and how long this will take
- Your financial situation
- Why you need to be given certain assets or property
- Items of marital property your spouse has taken
- Your ex's failure to pay temporary alimony or child support
- Why a certain item should be considered marital or separate property, or why a debt should be considered marital or separate debt
- Information about a business your ex owns

Note that this form does not include a section for custody. See Chapter 16 for more information about preparing your testimony for a custody trial.

Preparing for Your Spouse's Witnesses

Your spouse will present witnesses in court, just as you do. After his or her attorney is done questioning them, your attorney will have the opportunity to do so. This is called *cross-examination*. It is your turn to get more information from the witnesses or to show that they are leaving facts out, not being truthful, or clouding reality.

Take some time to think about the witnesses your spouse might call. Sometimes attorneys exchange witness lists during the discovery phase, but this does not happen all the time—or even most of the time. This is a choice your attorney will make. If witness lists are exchanged, ask your attorney for a copy of your spouse's list and use that when you prepare your cross-examination notes. If lists are not exchanged, you may hear through the grapevine or make some educated guesses about friends and relatives who have been subpoenaed or asked to testify. You can expect your spouse to testify as well.

Prepare the Cross-Examination Notes worksheet by first filling in the names of witnesses you are sure will be called or who are on the witness list obtained by your attorney. Then write down what they know, how they can hurt your case (be honest here), things you know about them that make them look bad, and information they have that will be helpful to your case. It is important to be honest about what these witnesses know. You want your attorney to be prepared in the courtroom, not surprised. It can be hard to be forthright about things that have happened or things you've done in your marriage, but you will have the best chance at a good outcome if you disclose them completely to your attorney, talk about how they might come out, and formulate a plan for dealing with them.

Print an extra blank copy of the Cross-Examination Notes worksheet and take it to court with you in case your spouse calls any witnesses you did not anticipate. Use this copy to make notes of anything untrue these witnesses say, facts they leave out, and issues your attorney should ask about on cross-examination. The court may grant your attorney a few minutes to meet with you before cross-examining a surprise witness, and you can share the information then; if not, you can pass the page to your attorney while he or she is questioning the witness.

Physical Evidence

If you've learned anything from this book, it's probably the fact that paperwork and documents are key to the divorce process. You probably bought this book to help organize all that paperwork. And as much as these documents are an important type of evidence, some cases require evidence beyond paper. The following sections will discuss the types of physical evidence (other than documents and papers) that you might need in your case. Create a list of evidence using the Physical Evidence List.

Photographs

Photographs can provide persuasive evidence. You may use them to show many things:

- Your history as a parent (through a photo album)
- Your spouse's mistreatment of you or your children
- Conditions that exist in either home (such as mold, dirt, safety hazards, or overcrowding in your ex's home or the good conditions in your own)
- Proof that certain assets or belongings exist (that new truck your ex is hiding behind his father's garage)
- The value of some belongings or assets (a set of antique glass that may sound expensive but actually is chipped and cracked; a vacation home that sounds valuable but is actually a rundown cabin)

- Damage done by your spouse to marital assets
- Proof of certain activities by your spouse (working a second job or removing assets from the marital home)
- Changes in the value of property (particularly useful when you are claiming you helped increase the value of your ex's separate property, with before and after shots showing the changes)

Photographs can be compelling evidence, because they show the judge in full color what you are trying to prove. They offer clear visual images that often have more impact than testimony by a witness.

Photographs cannot be submitted to the court alone, however. To enter a photograph into evidence, your attorney must have the photographer available to testify. The person who took the photo must testify that he or she took the photo, that it is an accurate representation of whatever it shows, and that it has not been altered.

If you have photographs to give your attorney, you can print them out and label them on the back or send them digitally. Include a caption or label indicating when each was taken, by whom, and who or what is in it; alternatively, you can number each photo and create a corresponding written list containing the relevant information. It is a good idea to keep copies of photographs, because if they are entered into evidence, you may not get them back. If you're using digital photos, keep copies of them on a jump drive or an external hard drive someplace where it cannot be accidentally deleted.

Videos

Video can be another compelling kind of evidence. It can reveal a person's character or behavior in a way photographs cannot, because it shows the person in action. If you submit a video to your attorney, be sure to label it with the date and what it shows. Keep a digital copy in a safe place. Some courts will require testimony by the person who shot the tape or was in control of the camera to ensure that the video has not been tampered with.

Don't bother submitting a video unless it shows something important. A video of a child's dance recital or a birthday party won't impress a judge, but one that shows the way a parent treats that child or captures a significant and revealing event could be useful. If you have both photos and video, let your attorney know and he or she will select which to use.

Voice Recordings

Some people record conversations with their spouses without realizing that it is illegal in many states to record another person without his or her permission. To find out what the laws are in your state, visit http://www.rcfp.org/taping or contact your attorney. When submitting recordings to your attorney, be sure to label them with dates and the names of the people who are on them. Voice recordings will be of interest only if they provide substantive evidence or an important admission by your spouse.

Other Physical Evidence

Other nondocument types of physical evidence your attorney might be able to use include the following:

- Items broken or damaged by your spouse
- Ripped, filthy, or bloody clothing (yours or your child's) to show abuse or neglect
- Computer jump drives
- Computer file evidence of child pornography
- Answering machine or voice mail messages

Note that you should *not* steal or hide items—such as your ex's phone, his or her computer, or separate property—to use as evidence.

When presenting physical evidence, someone (you or another witness) with direct knowledge of the item must testify. When you give physical evidence to your attorney, include a written explanation of what the item is, its significance, and who the appropriate witness might be.

How to Find Evidence

All the evidence you provide to your attorney must be tied to some issue in the case, so the first thing to think about is what you're trying to prove. Don't bother with evidence about things everyone agrees on. Here are some examples of issues that might need to be proven:

- Your spouse is a bad parent.
- You are a wonderful parent.
- Your children have special needs.
- Your spouse destroyed marital assets.
- You gave up getting your degree to support your spouse and take care of your kids.
- Your spouse threatened or harmed you.
- You spent weeks renovating the home your ex owned before you were married.
- Your spouse is not fully disclosing income or assets.

Using the Physical Evidence

Use the Physical Evidence List at the end of this chapter to clarify what each piece of evidence can prove about you or your spouse. Then gather the evidence you need when your spouse is not around. If you fear repercussions from your spouse, discuss your concerns with your attorney.

You can snoop around to find things that might help your case, but the final call as to whether something is useful should be left up to your attorney. Your job is to provide him or her with as much information and evidence as possible. Then stand aside as he or she decides what can legally be used and what fits into the strategy for your case.

LIST OF POSSIBLE WITNESSES

Name	Topics

WITNESS WORKSHEET

Create one worksheet for each witness.

Name _____

Age _____

Address _____

Phone _____

E-mail address _____

Employment _____

Relationship _____

Information witness can provide:

_____

_____

_____

_____

_____

_____

_____

_____

_____

_____

_____

_____

_____

_____

_____

_____

_____

_____

NOTES FOR YOUR TESTIMONY

Make notes on these pages about what you can testify to.

Alimony

_____

_____

_____

_____

_____

_____

Child Support

_____

_____

_____

_____

_____

_____

_____

Property and Debt Division
(You do not need to re-create your list of disputed items from Chapter 11.
Instead, explain why you should get certain items.)

_____

_____

_____

_____

_____

_____

continued ▶

Reason for Divorce

_____

_____

_____

_____

_____

_____

Other

_____

_____

_____

_____

_____

_____

_____

_____

_____

_____

_____

_____

_____

_____

_____

_____

_____

_____

_____

CROSS-EXAMINATION NOTES

Print copies of this log for further use.

Witness's Name _____

_____
_____
_____
_____
_____
_____
_____
_____
_____
_____
_____
_____
_____
_____
_____
_____
_____
_____
_____
_____
_____
_____
_____
_____
_____
_____
_____
_____

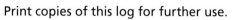
Print copies of this log for further use.

Description	What It Can Prove

16

Custody Trials

If you're going to have a trial about custody, prepare yourself for some serious mud-slinging. This is often the nastiest, most painful, and most emotional part of a divorce proceeding. You and your spouse will each try to show the court that you are a terrific parent and that the other person is a terrible parent. Sometimes these trials involve big issues such as abuse or neglect, but most of the time they deal with tiny pieces—child care, day-to-day activities, and particular events—that can be painstaking to put together.

There are two types of custody trials. Some couples have similar ideas about how to arrange custody and visitation but simply can't agree on the details. This impasse sometimes leads to a visitation trial in which the emphasis is on schedules—how your time should be shared with your children and what division is the best for them. Other couples have knock-down, drag-out custody battles in which each wants to be the residential parent or the parent with sole custody, cutting the other out of the picture as much as possible. These complicated cases involve a lot of evidence and testimony about parenting abilities and events.

This chapter helps you gather evidence and record behavior so that your attorney can convince the court that your position on custody or visitation is the right one.

Documenting the Past

Although the court is going to place the most emphasis on the current parenting arrangement, the past is important too. Most parents are on their best behavior while the case is pending, but you want to show what things were like before you came to court. Take some time to reconstruct what you can of the last few months or the last year. Use your personal calendar or the family calendar for this purpose. Go through and highlight dates your spouse was out of town or worked long hours and could not spend time with the kids. Highlight special events, recitals, sports events, and so on that he or she missed.

You may need to go even further back if something important occurred in the past—if you took a year off to be home with the kids, for example, or if you missed a lot of time at work to care for a sick child. If you've been the one who always has taken the children to medical, dental, hair, and orthodontic appointments or things like lessons or practices, make a note of this and indicate how many years this has been the case. Use the Parenting Journal form at the end of this chapter to write out important situations from the past that demonstrate your ongoing commitment to parenting. Write down anything that shows a distinct pattern of parenting responsibilities over the past few years.

Documenting Your Own Parenting Abilities

It may seem difficult to step back and look objectively at your own parenting abilities, but you need to do so in order to build your case, because after all, this is what the judge is going to do. Go through your calendar for the past few months and note all the times you were there for your children—events, games, practices, medical appointments, time off from work when they were sick, and so on. Fill in special little things you did with them: maybe you took them on a long bike ride over the Memorial Day weekend or went to a movie on a weeknight in January. Maybe you did a special craft with them for Valentine's Day or helped with a science project. Fill in what you can recall.

Continue to keep accurate records about parenting. Your calendar will be your essential tool for doing this. Record every activity you participate in with your children. Put down the times you drive them places. Make notes about different places you take them or major things you do together. It may seem like a lot of effort to record all of this, but the more you can document, the better your case will be.

Use the Child Care Checklist to document the things you usually do for your children. Not only is the list useful for your attorney, but it can also be persuasive if you are trying to convince your spouse to settle—it may provide overwhelming evidence that you do most things for your kids, and your spouse will feel it's going to be an obvious case when presented to the judge. Check off the things that you routinely do or supervise as a parent. Leave blank those items that your spouse usually handles. Cross off items that do not apply to your child (such as diapers or activities that no longer require your supervision if your children are older). If some things are shared equally, place a *J* next to them for "joint." Then look at the list. If you have checked most of the items, then you are the one who has been primarily involved in the day-to-day care of your children. If most items have a *J*, then you and your spouse have truly been equal partners in parenting, and a joint parenting arrangement might work best. If you have left most items blank, it means your spouse has done most of the day-to-day child care and supervision. This doesn't mean you can't get custody of your child, but it does mean that the family is more accustomed to your spouse handling the daily arrangements.

You should probably not give this checklist to your attorney if it does not show you taking on most of the child care responsibilities. However, if you are only seeking visitation and your spouse is opposing it, a checklist that shows moderate involvement can be helpful. This list can also be used to help you ramp up your involvement as a parent. You might never have realized how the division of parenting responsibilities really fell in your family, but if you see how much you haven't been involved in, this could be a catalyst for you to make some changes.

If certain parenting responsibilities have changed, make a note of this in the margin of the checklist. For example, perhaps you drove your child to elementary school every day for six years, but he or she now walks to middle school. Or maybe you are the parent of a two-year-old who recently became potty trained, but you are the one who was primarily responsible for diapers and potty training. These notes can help your attorney see a pattern of who is taking on parenting responsibilities.

Write in any responsibilities not included on this list that are part of your life.

Focusing on the Other Parent's Faults

If you're going to win a custody case, you've got to present information about the other parent in a way that convinces the judge that you are the person the children should spend most of their time with. This doesn't mean complete character assassination, but it does mean you need to document anything that shows your spouse's parenting abilities in a negative light. Of course, you should never set out to prove something that you know isn't true.

In pointing out your spouse's shortcomings, focus on facts that affect his or her parenting abilities rather than general lifestyle issues. Many parents, for example, are quick to point out that their spouse has a new girlfriend or boyfriend. In actuality, the court is interested in this new partner only if the relationship has a negative impact on the children. If the children don't have much contact with the new partner, or if they do see the person a lot but it's not a negative situation, the court won't care. Additionally, if your ex is gay, the court doesn't care (although there are still some older judges on the bench who may harbor prejudice) as long as there is no impact on your kids, just as with a new partner of the opposite sex. The judge doesn't care if your spouse is a lying, scheming rat toward you as long as he or she is not that way with the children. It is possible to be a horrible spouse yet be a good parent at the same time, and this can be hard to accept while you are still healing from the end of your relationship. Your ex's personality traits, lifestyle choices, and actions matter in the custody trial only if they have a negative impact on the children.

Use the Spouse's Parenting Abilities form to write down incidents that demonstrate the problems your spouse has as a parent. Incidents that might be significant include things such as the following:

- Failing to give your child necessary medication
- Refusing to learn about your child's disability or treatment for medical conditions
- Physically punishing or abusing your child (While it's not illegal to spank a child, many judges frown on this.)
- Not properly supervising your child, leading to injury or dangerous situations
- Driving while intoxicated with your child in the car or driving while using a cell phone
- Leaving your child with inappropriate sitters
- Picking your child up late from school or activities

155

- Missing important events in your child's life, like recitals, graduations, birthdays, holidays, and more
- Not using visitation time to actually be with your child
- Not taking care of your child's basic hygiene or nutrition
- Failing to use basic safety precautions like car seats, childproofing, and so on
- Causing arguments or being abusive to you in front of your child

While your take on the situation is important, think about other people who can second your opinion. Have friends, relatives, or neighbors observed the behaviors that you noted? See Chapter 15 for more information about compiling a witness list.

Parenting Classes

Some courts routinely refer (meaning attendance is recommended but not required) all divorcing parents to classes or seminars about how to coparent after a divorce and how to manage visitation moving forward. If you are referred to this kind of program, go even if your spouse is not planning on doing so. Your attendance is reported to the court and will cast you in a better light. And the class is likely to be helpful to you, even if your spouse does not participate. A judge in some states can require participation in a parenting class, and failure to comply is contempt of court.

If there is a question about one parent's ability to care for children, the court may order (require) him or her to attend a parenting skills class. If this happens to you, don't be insulted—think of it as an opportunity to show the court that you are reliable, trustworthy, proactive, and responsible. If you really don't need the class, then you will complete it easily with flying colors and may be able to get a good recommendation from the instructor. If you are adamant about not attending these classes, the alternative is to have your attorney obtain a professional evaluation of your parenting skills (which you will have to pay for) by a psychologist or therapist who is trained in making these kinds of judgments. This professional will provide a report that the court will rely on in evaluating your abilities.

If you believe your spouse seriously lacks parenting skills, talk to your lawyer about requesting parenting classes or a parenting evaluation for him or her.

Keeping Your Kids Out of It

It is tempting to rely on information you get from your children to help you win a custody case, but that information is often unreliable. Parents get upset when children return from the other parent's home and talk about what they did, what the parent did or said, or problems that occurred. Remember that your children will almost always try to play one parent against the other and will be encouraged by your obvious reactions. They want to please you or get a reaction out of you, and if telling you unflattering things about the other parent accomplishes that, they will continue to do so and may even make things up.

If you've ever heard your children describe an event you all attended, you know that children usually don't report accurately. When a child reports things, facts that you think are important can often be left out, and minor details can become important parts of the story. A child's-eye view is not always accurate! Keep this in mind when your children come home from spending time with the other parent and tell you things. You need to sift through the information and find out what really happened. It can often be helpful to talk to the other parent, because there is usually a simple explanation that the kids have left out. Keep in mind that kids love to embellish things, particularly if they can see that you're interested.

It is tempting to pump your children for information after they spend time with your ex, but it's a bad idea. Although you are trying to build your case, you have to respect your children's right to a relationship with the other parent. They are not spies for either of you, and placing them in that position can only be damaging. If you are always asking your kids for details about what your spouse did or said, they are going to feel pressured. They don't want to let you down and are likely to come up with things to tell you. At the same time, they will feel guilty about betraying the other parent. It creates a situation that causes a lot of anxiety. Divorce is hard enough for your children without being placed in the middle of the dispute.

That being said, sometimes there are things you learn from your child that you just can't ignore. If he or she comes home and tells you, "Mommy hit me," or "Daddy wouldn't let me go to my basketball game," you know there's a problem. The key here is not to jump to conclusions. You may not be getting the full story. Details have probably been left out that could change your take on it. Consider asking your ex about what happened. If you're satisfied with his or her explanation, let it go. If you're not satisfied—or if these situations occur repeatedly and your spouse has an excuse for each one—it's time to create a record.

Use the Parenting Journal form to record things your children tell you, things your spouse tells you, and things you notice yourself. You can use the form in this book or just create your own computer file.

Siblings and Half-Siblings

A child's relationships with siblings are an important part of his or her life. While it is very rare for a court to separate siblings, a judge might consider a suggestion to split them up. If you're worried about it, take steps to document how important the children are to each other. Use your Parenting Journal to record how they spend their time together and how they relate to each other.

If you have children from a prior marriage or relationship, they are equally important in the lives of your children from this marriage. If the half-siblings are with you only part of the time (because of the parenting plan you have with the other parent), offer a clear schedule of when they are with you so you can ensure that the court-appointed visitation schedule allows the children from this marriage time with their half-siblings. Again, you should document the time they spend together, what they do, and how important they are to each other.

PARENTING JOURNAL

Use this form to record impressions about custody and visitation, things your children or spouse might say, and details about what happened on certain days or in certain situations that might support your position on custody and visitation. You should also include information about your activities and responsibilities as a parent now and in the past, so that you can show a pattern of your involvement on a daily basis.

_____
_____
_____
_____
_____
_____
_____
_____
_____
_____
_____
_____
_____
_____
_____
_____
_____
_____
_____
_____
_____
_____
_____
_____
_____

CHILD CARE CHECKLIST

Use this checklist to document things you usually do for your children. If your children are not close in age, it can be useful to prepare one form per child.

1. Hygiene

☐ Giving baths

☐ Getting haircuts (either doing them or taking the child for them)

☐ Cleaning hands and face

☐ Dressing

☐ Brushing teeth

☐ Flossing

☐ Doing laundry

☐ Changing sheets

☐ Doing diaper changes/bathroom use/potty training

☐ Purchasing clothing, shoes, equipment, and uniforms

☐ Combing/styling hair

☐ Caring for nails

☐ Cleaning child's room

☐ Cleaning child's bathroom

☐ Cleaning up child after meals

2. Meals and Food

☐ Cooking meals

☐ Feeding meals

☐ Making snacks

☐ Packing lunches or snacks for school or day care

☐ Cleaning up

☐ Preparing and sending food items to school events (birthday, parties, and so on)

☐ Planning meals

☐ Shopping

☐ Teaching the child to cook

3. Sleep

☐ Supervising bedtime rituals

☐ Supervising naps

☐ Handling nighttime wake-ups

☐ Handling morning wake-ups

4. Education

☐ Reading to the child

☐ Attending parent-teacher conferences

☐ Helping with homework

☐ Helping with school projects

☐ Attending school functions

☐ Doing educational activities at home

☐ Volunteering in the classroom or as a coach

159

continued ▶

4. Education, *continued*

☐ Being involved in extracurricular events, sports, and so on

☐ Transporting the child to/from school

☐ Transporting the child to/from activities

☐ Providing child care when the child is home sick

☐ Making trips to the library

☐ Making arrangements for extracurricular activities, sports, and so on

☐ Attending extracurricular activities, sports, and so on

☐ Taking trips to museums and other educational places

☐ Helping with arts and crafts projects

☐ Homeschooling

☐ Being involved with the PTO/PTA and other parent groups

☐ Teaching the child to walk

☐ Teaching the child to tie shoes

☐ Teaching the child to write his/her name

☐ Teaching the child to read

☐ Teaching the child to ride a bike

☐ Teaching the child to drive

☐ Other

5. Emotional Nurturing

☐ Rocking, soothing, and holding

☐ Talking and giving advice

☐ Building the child's self-esteem

☐ Participating in the child's interests

☐ Setting and enforcing rules and limits

☐ Comforting

6. Health Care

☐ Taking the child to health care appointments

☐ Calling health care providers for assistance

☐ Scheduling health care appointments

☐ Applying sunscreen

☐ Applying bug repellent

☐ Giving/supervising medication

☐ Handling health insurance claims

☐ Supervising use of a bicycle helmet

☐ Providing home medical care (cuts, stings, scrapes, headaches)

☐ Supervising home physical therapy or occupational therapy exercises

7. Entertainment and Play

☐ Driving the child to parties and playdates

☐ Buying toys

☐ Organizing and cleaning toys

☐ Supervising the child's friends at home

☐ Playing sports with the child

☐ Planning family vacations

☐ Watching TV/videos with the child

☐ Planning parties

☐ Playing games

☐ Playing with toys

☐ Purchasing gifts for the child

☐ Assisting the child with pet care

8. Other

☐ _____

☐ _____

☐ _____

☐ _____

SPOUSE'S PARENTING ABILITIES

Use this form to record actual incidents or general impressions of your spouse's parenting.

17

It's All Over! Now What?

Once your divorce is official, there will be loose ends to tie up and things you'll need to continue tracking. Your divorce is finalized once your attorney has filed or recorded the papers that have been signed by the judge. It may take a week or two after the judge's decision for it to be official. Make sure you get a copy of the final order. You may need to show it when making name changes and for your child's school.

Changing Your Name

Your divorce decree will include authorization to change your name if you changed your name when you married. Once the decree is final, you may resume using your premarital name or you can continue using your married name, if you wish. This is a matter of personal choice. You will need to show a copy of your divorce decree and marriage license when changing your name on official documents such as a driver's license, passport, or Social Security card. Your new driver's license will usually suffice as proof for other documents that require a name change. Use this checklist to ensure that you've changed your name in all the essential places:

- ☐ Bank accounts, including your PayPal account

- ☐ Car registration and insurance

- ☐ Children's schools or day care

- ☐ Club or gym memberships

- ☐ Credit cards

- ☐ Dental insurance (Ask for a new card.)

- [ ] Driver's license (Check your state department of motor vehicles website for forms and information.)

- [ ] Employer (Get a new ID card if your employer requires one and make sure your paychecks go to the name on your bank account.)

- [ ] Frequent flier programs and loyalty programs

- [ ] Health care providers who treat you and your children

- [ ] Health insurance (Get a new card.)

- [ ] Investments

- [ ] Library card

- [ ] Life insurance

- [ ] Newspaper and magazine subscriptions

- [ ] Online accounts and subscriptions, including your e-mail account

- [ ] Passport (visit http://travel.state.gov/passport/correcting/ChangeName/ChangeName_851.html)

- [ ] Pensions and retirement plans

- [ ] Social media

- [ ] Social Security card (visit http://ssa-custhelp.ssa.gov/app/answers/detail/a_id/315/~/change-a-name-on-a-social-security-card)

- [ ] Union

- [ ] Utility bills, including cell phone, Internet, and cable services

- [ ] Veterinarian

Updating Your Insurance

Remove your ex from your auto and homeowner's or renter's insurance policies. Make sure your policy now covers only the vehicle or property that is in your name and that your name is not on the policy for items your ex-spouse now owns. Change the beneficiary of your life insurance policy if it is currently your ex (unless the court has ordered you to continue it). Most people name their children when changing this.

If you will be receiving health insurance through your ex's plan under COBRA (see Chapter 13), complete the paperwork required by the carrier and your ex-spouse's employer, and find out how much the premiums will be and when they will be due each month. Ask if you will receive a bill or if you are responsible for making payments on your own. Mark the due dates on your calendar. Find out when you are no longer eligible for COBRA coverage and mark that date on your calendar as well. Also make a note to yourself six months before that date to start seeking new coverage. It's important to do this well in advance, because most health care plans have enrollment periods only two to four times a year.

If you will be issued a new card for the COBRA coverage, get that as quickly as possible and provide it to all of your health care providers. If you and your children will now be on different health insurance plans, make sure you have a copy of the card that covers them.

Protecting Your Credit

Make sure you have closed or frozen all joint credit cards. Open new accounts in your own name. Obtain a copy of your credit report (https://www.annualcreditreport.com) about three to five months after your divorce is finalized and check for joint accounts. If any still appear on the report, close them in writing. Some accounts that you closed may still appear as open on your report. Contact the credit reporting agency and ask that their status be changed.

If your ex had access to the account numbers of your separate credit card accounts, it's a good idea to ask that those account numbers be changed. Be sure to change your bank account information if you pay your credit card bills online and are now paying from a different account.

Dividing Assets

When your divorce is finalized, your court order will specify how everything (or the majority of your marital assets) is to be divided between you and your ex-spouse. If you each still have personal property that belongs to the other, you'll want to exchange it as soon as possible. If your ex is not cooperative, let your attorney know. He or she will contact your ex's attorney to make sure it gets done. Use the Receipts for Property Distribution at the end of this chapter to keep track of what has been exchanged. Do not dispose of your ex's property! Talk with your attorney if it's still lying around weeks later. It is tempting to get it all out of your life, but you want to be sure you aren't later held in contempt of court.

You'll also need to get ownership changed on larger items that were owned jointly and will now be in your name alone. For cars and boats, you'll need a copy of the title and of the divorce decree. Contact your state department of motor vehicles for title transfer information. Houses are more complicated. You can get the deed changed (your lawyer can handle this for you), which indicates ownership, but changing the mortgage will usually require you to refinance it in the name of the sole owner (otherwise, you both remain liable for it in the eyes of the bank). Even if the court orders one of you to be responsible for the mortgage, the bank is not required to follow this and can still sue you if your ex fails to make payments. It is possible to ask the bank to provide a release to the person the court has said is no longer responsible for the mortgage, but the bank has no incentive to do this, and it is a rare occurrence. When dealing with bank accounts and investments, it is simplest to close the joint accounts and roll the money into individual accounts.

If you will be selling your home or other large assets, you will need to work together to do so. You must agree on whether or not to accept offers, and you will both need to sign paperwork to complete the sale.

If there is going to be a division of a retirement account or pension, your attorney will handle the paperwork involved in this, which can be very complicated and time-consuming. A document called a qualified domestic relations order (QDRO) needs to be completed and signed by the court to get the company holding the account to release the funds.

Leases

If you and your ex-spouse rented your residence and you are now the sole occupant, contact your landlord and amend the lease to include only your name. Leaving your ex's name on the lease will make him or her responsible for rent (which might not bother you), but it will also give him or her the legal right to access the apartment (something you don't want). If you're moving out, be sure you're no longer financially responsible for rent and that your name is removed from the lease. It will be up to the landlord to agree to remove a name from the lease, but most do not have an issue with doing so.

Your Will

Once your divorce is final, you will need to change your will. If you had a will while you were married, it probably named your ex as a beneficiary. You probably want to change that now. Think carefully about how you would like to distribute your belongings. If you have children and you are the parent they live with most, you will need to name a guardian for them in case you die while they are still minors and you do not want your ex to have custody. In the event of your death, the court will consider your choice of guardian but will make the final decision. Preference is usually given to the other parent unless there is a very good reason not to.

Talk to your attorney about changing your will. He or she may be able to do this for you or can refer you to an attorney who can.

Health Care Directives

If you have not already done so, make sure you change your health care directives (also called a health care proxy, living will, or health care power of attorney) so that your ex no longer has the ability to make health care decisions for you if you are ill and can't decide for yourself. If you have given copies of this document to your doctor, be sure to give him or her the new document and ask for the old one back. You will want to destroy all copies of the old version.

Wedding and Relationship Mementos

Now that your marriage is over, you probably have mixed feelings about things like your wedding photos, wedding dress, wedding ring, or keepsakes. Some people feel the need to get rid of it all. Others recognize that these things represent happy times (even if they didn't last) and are an important part of their personal history. However you feel about it, it's your choice, and there is no wrong answer.

If you have children, consider their feelings about these items. Your marriage is important to them, and they may want to have your wedding photos, dress, or rings sometime in the future. Photographs of their parents together will have meaning to them, because these are part of their family history.

If you do decide to get rid of things like your wedding ring or dress, consider reselling them to make some extra cash (many jewelry shops will purchase gold, and you can sell the dress on eBay, Craigslist, or at a consignment shop). Some women have the diamond from their engagement ring reset as a pendant or earrings. The gold can also be melted down and used to create another piece of jewelry.

Coping with Your Feelings

When your divorce becomes final, you will probably experience a wide range of feelings, including relief, sadness, joy, depression, independence, anger, resentment, or grief. All of these reactions are normal, and your feelings will probably change as you go along. Your reaction to your divorce doesn't end with the final decision in the case. Adjusting to a different life is a long and difficult process, and you shouldn't feel that you need to follow a timetable. Many people find that the actual divorce process has kept their minds occupied and that the postdivorce period is unexpectedly more difficult. Don't be afraid to seek counseling if you need it.

Continuing to Track Payments

You will need to continue tracking child support and alimony payments. Print copies of the Ongoing Child Support Log and the Ongoing Alimony Log at the end of this chapter and complete them regularly. Also print copies of the Child Support Receipts and Alimony Receipts and use them for ongoing payments.

When you transfer property or assets according to the divorce decree, get a receipt for items that will not leave a paper trail on their own. For example, when you roll a mutual fund over from joint names to your ex-spouse, there is a record of this. But when you give your ex $500 cash or expensive photography equipment, there will be no paper trail unless you create one. Ask your ex-spouse to sign a receipt indicating acceptance of the item. Use the Receipts for Property Distribution at the end of this chapter.

Problems with Payments

If your ex fails to make alimony or child support payments, you should contact your attorney. If child support payments are being made through the state, the child support collection agency will handle enforcement and collection. If not, it's up to you and your attorney to collect. Collection can be a long process and involve returning to court many times. It's important that you keep good records so your evidence will be clear.

Attorney Bills

You will likely receive a final bill from your attorney once your case has ended. Make sure the retainer you paid was deducted. If you went to trial, your bill may be quite high. If you haven't already done so, talk to your attorney about a payment plan. Be sure to ask for an itemized bill that shows what portion of your bill may be tax deductible.

Remember that it's your attorney's job to complete all of the final paperwork involved in your divorce. If you don't get the documents you need, call and ask for them.

Maintaining Your Household

Whether you are remaining in the marital home after your divorce or are moving to a new residence, you have to take stock of your household. Lots of things have changed, and this is a time for reassessment. It makes sense to wait a while before running out and replacing everything your ex got in the divorce. Maybe you'll find that you really have no need for some of those items anymore. Start with the essentials and then see what else you want.

It can be expensive to re-equip your household. Try these money-saving ideas:

- Go to yard sales or garage sales.
- Visit secondhand stores.
- Ask friends and relatives for things they don't want.
- Shop warehouse clubs.
- Watch for sales, discounts, and rebates.
- Compare prices using apps like RedLaser and Amazon Price Check.
- Shop on eBay.

- Check Craigslist or Freecycle for items people are giving away.
- Don't replace things unless you really need them.

You'll find that once you're on your own, you can change many things about the way you live, since you have no one to answer to but yourself. Try out new things and new routines. Many people discover surprising new sides to themselves after a divorce.

Managing Finances

You now have the freedom to change not only how you live, but also how you manage your finances. You are now solely responsible for all spending and earning in your household. This can be a burden or a great freedom. Learn to budget your money and expenses so you have a clear idea of how much you can spend. Once you adjust to your new lifestyle, start thinking about the future. You are now completely responsible for your own retirement, so start considering how you will manage it. It's also important to start a rainy-day fund so you can manage unexpected expenses or emergencies that may arise.

When you file your taxes, you can file as single or as single head of household for the first calendar year in which you are not married and then the years after that. Before then, you will need to consult with your tax adviser about how you will file for the calendar year in which you were married and then divorced. Make sure you are clear as to whether you or your ex will be claiming the children as dependents, as discussed in Chapter 12.

Important Documents for Your Children

If you are the parent with residential custody, make sure you are in possession of the following items for each child:

- Birth certificate
- Baptismal certificate, bris certificate, or other religious records
- Passport
- Social Security card
- Bank statements/password for accounts in the child's name
- Life insurance policies
- Immunization records
- Important medical records
- Health insurance cards

If you do not have residential custody of your children, make sure you do the following:

- Contact your children's schools and the leaders of their extracurricular activities and arrange to receive separate copies/e-mails of report cards, notices of events and games, calendars, and schedules for parent-teacher conferences.
- Notify your children's medical care providers that you have the authority to seek treatment for your kids (you may need to provide copies of your custody papers), and arrange for separate updates on your children's health, if necessary. If you do not have joint legal custody, your ex may need to complete an authorization allowing you to obtain medical care for your children when they are with you.
- Keep copies of each child's health insurance card, birth certificate, and Social Security card.

RECEIPTS FOR PROPERTY DISTRIBUTION

Print copies of these receipts so you can fill them out whenever property is exchanged.

Property Receipt

I received the following item _____

from _____ on _____ [date] as part of the property

distribution agreement order.

_____

[signature]

Property Receipt

I received the following item _____

from _____ on _____ [date] as part of the property

distribution agreement order.

_____

[signature]

Property Receipt

I received the following item _____

from _____ on _____ [date] as part of the property

distribution agreement order.

_____

[signature]

ONGOING CHILD SUPPORT LOG

Print copies of this log so you can continue to track child support payments.

Date	Check Number	Amount	Payment Period	Check if Unpaid

ONGOING ALIMONY LOG

Print copies of this log so you can continue to track alimony payments.

Date	Check Number	Amount	Payment Period	Check if Unpaid

Print several copies of this page so you can prepare a receipt for each month.

Child Support Receipt

I received $_____ from _____ on _____ [date]

for the period of _____ to _____ as child support.

_____

[signature]

Child Support Receipt

I received $_____ from _____ on _____ [date]

for the period of _____ to _____ as child support.

_____

[signature]

Child Support Receipt

I received $_____ from _____ on _____ [date]

for the period of _____ to _____ as child support.

_____

[signature]

Child Support Receipt

I received $_____ from _____ on _____ [date]

for the period of _____ to _____ as child support.

_____

[signature]

ALIMONY RECEIPTS

Print copies of this page so you can fill out a receipt for every payment.

Alimony Receipt

I received $_____ from _____ on _____ [date]

for the period of _____ to _____ as alimony.

_____

[signature]

Alimony Receipt

I received $_____ from _____ on _____ [date]

for the period of _____ to _____ as alimony.

_____

[signature]

Alimony Receipt

I received $_____ from _____ on _____ [date]

for the period of _____ to _____ as alimony.

_____

[signature]

Alimony Receipt

I received $_____ from _____ on _____ [date]

for the period of _____ to _____ as alimony.

_____

[signature]

Resources

Organizations

American Academy of Matrimonial Lawyers
150 N. Michigan Ave., Suite 1420, Chicago, IL 60601
312-263-6477
http://www.aaml.org

American Association for Marriage and Family Therapy
112 S. Alfred St., Alexandria, VA 22314-3061
703-838-9808
http://www.aamft.org

American Bar Association
740 15th St. NW, Washington, DC 20005-1019
202-662-1000
http://www.abanet.org

American Counseling Association
5999 Stevenson Ave., Alexandria, VA 22304
800-347-6647
http://www.counseling.org

American Psychological Association
750 First St. NE, Washington, DC 20002-4242
800-374-2721
http://www.apa.org

Association for Conflict Resolution
12100 Sunset Hills Rd., Suite #130, Reston, VA 20190
703-234-4141
http://www.acrnet.org

Children's Rights Council
9470 Annapolis Road, Suite 310, Lanham, MD 20706
301-459-1220
http://www.crckids.org

Coalition for Collaborative Divorce
P.O. Box 1945, Agoura Hills, CA 91376-1945
800-559-3724
http://www.nocourtdivorce.com

Equifax (credit reporting agency)
P.O. Box 740241, Atlanta, GA 30374
800-685-1111
http://www.equifax.com

Experian (credit reporting agency)
P.O. Box 2104, Allen, TN 75013-2104
888-397-3742
http://www.experian.com

National Child Support Enforcement Association
1760 Old Meadow Rd., Suite 500, McLean, VA 22102
703-506-2880
http://www.ncsea.org

National Family Resiliency Center, Inc. (formerly Children of Separation and Divorce Center)
2000 Century Plaza, Suite 121, Columbia, MD 21044
410-740-9553
http://www.divorceabc.com

Parents Without Partners
1650 Dixie Highway, Suite 510, Boca Raton, FL 33432
561-391-8833
http://www.parentswithoutpartners.org

Supervised Visitation Network
3955 Riverside Ave., Jacksonville, FL 32205
904-419-7861
http://www.svnetwork.net

Trans Union (credit reporting agency)
Consumer Disclosure Center, P.O. Box 1000, Chester, PA 19022
http://www.transunion.com

Websites

Alimony (laws by state): http://family.findlaw.com/divorce/alimony/

American Responsible Divorce Network: http://www.responsible-divorce.com

Annual Credit Report: https://www.annualcreditreport.com

Appraiser USA (home appraisal): http://appraiserusa.com

Ball Park Business Valuation tool: http://www.bulletproofbizplans.com/BallPark

Banana Splits Resource Center (children's divorce support): http://www.banana splitsresourcecenter.org

Budgeting (consumer credit): http://www.consumercredit.com/budget-sheet.htm

Child Psychology (American Academy of Child & Adolescent Psychology): http://www.aacap.org/cs/root/facts_for_families/children_and_divorce

Child Support Calculator: http://www.childsupport.com/calculator.asp

Child Support Calculators (by state): http://www.alllaw.com/calculators /childsupport

Childhelp (national child abuse prevention): http://www.childhelp.org

Children and Divorce: http://www.childrenanddivorce.com

Divorce Advice and Help for Women: http://www.womansdivorce.com

Divorce and Children: http://www.divorceandchildren.com

Divorce Central: http://www.divorcecentral.com

Divorce Forms by State: http://family.findlaw.com/divorce/divorce-forms-by-state .html

Divorce Laws (by state): http://family.findlaw.com/divorce/divorce-laws/

Divorce Source: http://www.divorcesource.com

Divorce Support: http://www.divorcesupport.com

DivorceCare: http://www.divorcecare.com

DivorceCare for Kids: http://www.dc4k.org

How to Choose a Therapist: http://www.goodtherapy.org/blog/how-to-find-a -therapist/

Internal Revenue Service (tax responsibility for divorced individuals): http://www.irs .gov/publications/p504/ar02.html

Kelley Blue Book (car value): http://www.kbb.com

Making Lemonade—The Single Parent Network: http://www.makinglemonade.com

Mediators, Arbitrators, and Everything ADR: http://www.Mediate.com

National Coalition Against Domestic Violence: http://www.ncadv.org

Office of Child Support Enforcement: http://www.acf.hhs.gov/programs/css

Official Postal Service Change of Address Form: https://moversguide.usps.com/icoa /home/icoa-main-flow.do?execution=e1s1&_flowId=icoa-main-flow&

Realtor Finder: http://www.realtorfinder.com

Separated Parenting Access and Resource Center: http://www.deltabravo.net /custody

Single Parents: http://www.singleparents.about.com

State and Local Bar Associations: http://www.americanbar.org/groups/bar_services /resources/state_local_bar_associations.html

State Child Support Laws: http://family.findlaw.com/child-support/state-child -support-laws/

Where to Find Help for Your Child (American Academy of Child & Adolescent Psychology): http://www.aacap.org/cs/root/facts_for_families /where_to_find_help_for_your_child

Zillow—Valuation of Your Home: http://www.Zillow.com

Magazine

Divorce Magazine: http://www.divorcemag.com

Books for Adults

Ahrons, Constance. *The Good Divorce: Keeping Your Family Together When Your Marriage Comes Apart* (New York: HarperCollins, 1998).

Berry, Dawn Bradley. *The Divorce Recovery Sourcebook* (Lincolnwood, IL: NTC/Contemporary Books, 1999).

Clapp, Genevieve. *Divorce and New Beginnings: A Complete Guide to Recovery, Solo Parenting, Co-Parenting, and Stepfamilies* (New York: John Wiley & Sons, 2000).

Darnall, Douglas. *Divorce Casualties: Understanding Parental Alienation* (Lanham, MD: Taylor, 2008).

Emery, Robert. *The Truth About Children and Divorce: Dealing with the Emotions So You and Your Children Can Thrive* (New York: Viking, 2006).

Garrity Carla B., and Mitchell A. Baris. *Caught in the Middle: Protecting the Children of High-Conflict Divorce* (San Francisco, CA: Jossey-Bass, 1997).

Hannibal, Mary Ellen. *Good Parenting Through Your Divorce: How to Recognize, Encourage, and Respond to Your Child's Feelings and Help Them Get through Your Divorce* (New York: Marlowe & Co., 2002).

Grissom, Steve, and Kathy Leonard. *Divorce Care: Hope, Help, and Healing During and After Your Divorce* (Nashville, TN: Thomas Nelson, 2006).

Long, Nicholas, and Rex L. Forehand. *Making Divorce Easier on Your Child: 50 Effective Ways to Help Children Adjust* (Lincolnwood, IL: Contemporary Books, 2002).

Manfred, Erica, and Tina Tessina. *He's History, You're Not: Surviving Divorce After 40* (Guilford, CT: GPP Life, 2009).

McWade, Micki. *Getting Up, Getting Over, Getting On: A Twelve Step Guide to Divorce Recovery* (Beverly Hills, CA: Champion Press, 1999).

Mercer, Diana, and Marsha Kline Pruett. *Your Divorce Advisor: A Lawyer and a Psychologist Guide You Through the Legal and Emotional Landscape of Divorce* (New York: Fireside, 2001).

Neuman, M. Gary, and Patricia Romanowski. *Helping Your Kids Cope with Divorce the Sandcastles Way* (New York and Toronto: Random House, 1999).

Ross, Julia A., and Judy Corcoran. *Joint Custody with a Jerk: Raising a Child with an Uncooperative Ex* (New York: St. Martin's Press, 2011).

Sember, Brette. *The Complete Divorce Guide* (Clarence, NY: Sember Resources, 2012).

Sember, Brette. *Your Child, Custody, and the Law Guardian or Guardian ad litem* (Clarence, NY: Sember Resources, 2011).

Sember, Brette McWhorter. *How to Parent with Your Ex: Working Together for Your Child's Best Interest* (Naperville, IL: Sourcebooks, 2005).

Sember, Brette McWhorter. *No-Fight Divorce: Spend Less Money, Save Time, and Avoid Conflict Using Mediation* (Clarence, NY: Sember Resources, 2011).

Teyber, Edward. *Helping Children Cope with Divorce* (San Francisco, CA: Jossey-Bass, 2001).

Trafford, Abigail. *Crazy Time: Surviving Divorce and Building a New Life* (New York: HarperCollins, 1992).

Wallerstein, Judith S., and Sandra Blakeslee. *What About the Kids? Raising Your Children Before, During, and After Divorce* (New York: Hyperion Books, 2004).

Walther, Anne Newton. *Divorce Hangover: A Successful Strategy to End the Emotional Aftermath of Divorce* (San Francisco, CA: Tapestries, 2001).

Warshak, Richard A. *Divorce Poison: How to Protect Your Family from Bad-mouthing and Brainwashing* (New York: HarperCollins, 2010).

Books for Children

Bienenfeld, Florence. *My Mom and Dad Are Getting a Divorce!* (Miami: 1stBooks Library, 2002).

Brown, Laurene Krasny, and Marc Brown. *Dinosaurs Divorce: A Guide for Changing Families* (New York: Little, Brown & Company, 1988).

Holyoke, Nancy. *Help! A Girl's Guide to Divorce and Stepfamilies* (Middleton, WI: Pleasant Company Publications, 1999).

Lansky, Vicki. *It's Not Your Fault Koko Bear* (Deephaven, MN: Book Peddlers, 2003).

MacGregor, Cynthia. *The Divorce Helpbook for Teens* (Atascadero, CA: Impact, 2004).

Masurel, Claire. *Two Homes* (Somerville, MA: Candlewick Press, 2003).

Prokop, Michael S. *Divorce Happens to the Nicest Kids* (Warren, OH: Allegra House, 1996).

Ransom, Jeanie Franz. *I Don't Want to Talk About It* (Washington, DC: Magination, 2000).

Rogers, Fred. *Let's Talk About It: Divorce* (New York: Paper Star Book, 1998).

Schmitz, Tamara. *Standing on My Own Two Feet: A Child's Affirmation of Love in the Midst of Divorce* (New York: Price Stern Sloan, 2008).

Spelman, Cornelia Maude. *Mama and Daddy Bear's Divorce* (Park Ridge, IL: Albert Whitman, 1998).

Stern, Zoe, and Evan and Ellen Sue Stern. *Divorce Is Not the End of the World: Zoe's and Evan's Coping Guide for Kids* (Berkeley, CA: Tricycle, 2008).

Apps

Child Support: https://play.google.com/store/apps/details?id=air.com.California
.ChildSupport.Calculator&feature=search_result#?t=W251bGwsMSwxLDEsI
mFpci5jb20uQ2FsaWZvcm5pYS5DaGlsZFN1cHBvcnQuQ2FsY3VsYXRvciJd
Custody Connection: http://www.custodyconnection.com/
Divorce Log: https://itunes.apple.com/us/app/divorce-log/id483057414?mt=8
iSplit Divorce: https://itunes.apple.com/us/app/isplit-divorce/id548677092?mt=8
Kidganizer: http://www.kidganizer.com/
Our Family Wizard: http://www.ourfamilywizard.com/ofw/index.cfm/features
/iphone-app/

Index

11/13

DATE DUE

PRINTED IN U.S.A.

ADAMS FREE LIBRARY
92 Park Street
Adams, MA 01220-2096
413-743-8345